Transgender Inclusion

FOREWORD BY PEGGY RAJSKI FOUNDER OF THE TREVOR PROJECT

Transgender Inclusion

ALL THE THINGS YOU WANT TO ASK YOUR TRANSGENDER COWORKER

BUT SHOULDN'T

A.C. FOWLKES, PhD

WILEY

Published by John Wiley & Sons, Inc., Hoboken, New Jersey.
Published simultaneously in Canada.

For general information on our other products and services or for technical support, please contact our Customer Care Department within the United States at (800) 762-2974, outside the United States at (317) 572-3993 or fax (317) 572-4002.

Wiley also publishes its books in a variety of electronic formats. Some content that appears in print may not be available in electronic formats. For more information about Wiley products, visit our web site at www.wiley.com.

Library of Congress Cataloging-in-Publication Data is Available:

ISBN 9781394199259 (Cloth)
ISBN 9781394199266 (ePub)
ISBN 9781394199273 (ePDF)

Cover Design: PAUL MCCARTHY
Cover Art: © GETTY IMAGES | ARMAN ZHENIKEYEV
SKY10060349_111623

To Sherrie, the first boss I ever told that I was transgender

Contents

Foreword

A.C. Fowlkes – an experienced and highly respected consultant on DEIB (diversity, equity, inclusion, and belonging) for corporations, institutions of higher education, the prison system, and psychiatric hospitals – has written a thorough, inviting, and highly informative compendium of answers to the most frequently asked questions about what it's like to be trans.

His thoughtful, nuanced answers are informed not only by facts and figures from highly reputable research and resources, including the U.S. Trans Survey and the U.S. Census Bureau, but also by the deft blending of A.C.'s own lived experience as a trans man. Examples of his first-hand experiences are clear, focused, and balanced in just the right places throughout the book.

The gift of this book is that it creates a comfortable, safe place for cisgender workers and associates to get many of their most pressing questions answered about transgender colleagues:

- It lays out the essential basics – and differences – among medical, legal, and social transitioning.
- It explains the various reasons why certain trans individuals might choose one or some – though not

necessarily all – of these three options (medical, legal, or social) to feel they have successfully accomplished their own personal transition.

- The book devotes several helpful chapters to "dos and don'ts" of workplace etiquette.

- The book helps readers appreciate why greater understanding of their trans colleagues makes them even more valuable players in the world's increasingly diverse workplaces.

- While primarily focused on educating workers, the book is also an invaluable aid for managers, human resources, and other stakeholders in building a healthier, more effective, and ultimately more productive workplace environment.

- Framed as a guide for a cisgender populace, it can also be a useful reference for the transgender community in thinking about how to help their cisgender colleagues build better working relationships in the workplace.

This book will be a powerful, useful tool for years to come for cisgender workers and allies alike. Ultimately, I believe those who read the book thoroughly and take its points to heart can develop more comfortable, inclusive, and effective relationships both in and outside the workplace.

In fellowship and community,

—Peggy Rajski
Founder/Interim CEO
The Trevor Project

Introduction

Society as a whole is becoming increasingly aware of the transgender community. And while there is no shortage of opinions, there is a dearth of reliable, well-sourced information. To fill this gap, more and more companies are bringing in subject matter experts to demystify the process of creating an affirming environment for transgender employees and customers alike. Is bringing in a subject matter expert going to right every wrong? No. But it is a good place to start. I am one of those subject matter experts, and this book is my contribution to what is quickly becoming a robust conversation around transgender inclusion in the workplace.

Is it possible to create the safe and affirming workplace we so desire? I believe so. Is it possible to create a work environment in which you get it right 100% of the time? I'm not sure I would go quite that far. But, while I might fall short of believing in our ability to create a fully utopian workspace, I do believe we can do better than we currently are. And that process begins with the acquiring of knowledge, the furthering of understanding, and the application of both. It is my hope that this book will assist you in accomplishing just that.

Who This Book Is For

You might be wondering who the intended audience is for this book. Is this a book for transgender individuals? Is this a book for allies? Is this a book for both? Neither? Who is this book for, exactly? Well, the answer to that question is this book is for everyone who desires to learn more about the transgender community in general and how we might better support and hold space for them in the workplace in particular.

I do not purport to know all of the answers (or questions, for that matter). I will, however, speak openly about my experiences and make recommendations that are rooted not only in those experiences but in my understanding as a subject matter expert. I have no interest in converting you. I'm not even particularly sure what that would mean. My only desire in writing this is for you to leave knowing more than you did before you read the book and for you to be better prepared to work alongside your transgender colleagues.

So I'll not ask you if you are transgender or cisgender, if you are an ally, an advocate, or an accomplice. I'll not ask you about your political leanings or your religious affiliation. I'll not ask you any of that. But what I will ask you is if you have the tools that you need to be the best version of yourself when interacting with your transgender colleagues. If the answer to that question is anything less than a resounding yes, then this book was written with you in mind. How so? Glad you asked.

This book is for anyone interested in learning about the three widely recognized forms of transition: medical, social, and legal. This book is for anyone who wishes to better understand what policies and procedures are transgender-inclusive. This book is for anyone who would like to better understand the importance of utilizing a person's chosen name and pronouns. This book is for anyone who recognizes that there is value in all of us, even those who have historically (and presently) been pushed to the margins.

Whether you are an LGBTQ+ subject matter expert or know nothing of the community at all, this book was written with you in mind with enough information to provide a rudimentary or foundational understanding of the transgender community and enough nuance to take on higher-order discussions of means, access, and discrimination. This book can be utilized across sectors in that the instructions provided are universal enough to be folded into existing systems, but also specific enough to meet the needs of the transgender community in particular.

Whether you are a supervisor or a supervisee, this book is for you. Whether entry-level or the president and CEO, this book is for you. Whether you're a diversity equity and inclusion expert or know nothing of the topic, this book is for you. Whether you have personal access to the transgender community or do not personally know any member of the community, this book is for you. Whether you are cisgender or even transgender yourself, this book is for you.

Why This Book

What makes this book different is that it is written by a member of the transgender community who is a business professional and is currently undergoing the process of medical transition in the workplace. This book is not a nod to the hypothetical situations that one might find themselves in but is instead a direct reflection of my lived experience and the experiences of people I've had the great honor of working with. This book is different because it is written through a lens of belonging, and every recommendation I make will be to that end.

There are books on the market that focus on the transgender experience, but not many reflect on the transgender experience in the workplace. I have worked with some of the largest, most respected companies in the world. I have been brought into these organizations to answer questions about the transgender community in particular, and the LGBTQ+ community more broadly, and what I've brought to this book are some of the most common questions that I interface with, as well as some of the areas that I find people most often misunderstand.

So this book is your opportunity to learn from an LGBTQ+ sensitivity and transgender inclusion subject matter expert while also getting a chance to hear a little bit about my journey and what has been most effective for me along the way.

All of that said, this is not a memoir. This book will provide peeks into my personal experience, but it draws heavily on research and statistics, especially the U.S. Trans Survey and U.S. Census Bureau, but also other sources. While this book is meant to assist you in better relating to transgender people in the workplace, it is also meant to broaden your understanding of the transgender community as a whole. We are more than our experiences in the workplace, and this book seeks to highlight that.

What This Book Covers

This book provides a wide variety of information regarding the transgender community, from topics of frequent discussion and debate, such as what restroom a transgender person should be expected to use, to rarely discussed topics, like the impact that coming out as transgender has on the relationship between transgender individuals and their children.

After we discuss the transgender community more generally, we will dive into a discussion of the experiences of transgender individuals in the workplace. What's more, we will discuss frequently asked questions about transition, dos and don'ts in the workplace, and transgender-affirming policies and procedures. Lastly, we will discuss how to go about getting your questions answered if we didn't cover them in this book.

In terms of the structure of the book, Chapters 1 and 2 explore the transgender community and their workplace experiences. Chapters 3 through 6 examine the three types of transition (medical, legal, and social). Chapters 7 through 10 cover the dos and don'ts of transgender matters in the workplace, and Chapters 11 and 12 discuss how to build on all of this information and where to go from here.

Part I

Transgender Basics

Chapter 1

Getting to Know the Transgender Community

I think one of the most difficult balances to strike as a transgender person is the balance between novelty and normalcy. We are very much like you and not at all like you at the same time.

The transgender community is often misunderstood. Part of our very nature is the inherent dissonance between who others think we are and who we know ourselves to be. The writing of this chapter is particularly difficult because, while I want to highlight some of what we've come to know about the transgender community as a whole, I worry that such efforts can cast too wide a net. So as you read this chapter, please keep in mind that while these statistics speak to the lived experience of many transgender individuals in the United States and around the world, we are not homogeneous. We are beautiful. We are vibrant. We are nuanced. And we are often misunderstood.

But before discussing what we know about this community from a demographic standpoint, we must ensure that we understand what it means to be transgender. To do so, you must first understand the difference between sex assigned at birth and gender identity.

"It's a Boy!"

When a child is born, the sex assigned at birth is determined, and this determination usually takes place based almost solely on external anatomy. Whoever is in the room at the time of delivery, whether the doctor, the midwife, the doula, or whoever participates in the birthing process, is the one who determines the sex assigned at birth. Once a child is born, they look at the external anatomy, and they make a declaration as to the child's sex. In most instances, the child will be assigned either the sex of male or the sex of female based on the presentation of their genitalia. Sometimes a child will be assigned intersex instead of exclusively male or female, and this determination is typically based upon ambiguity in external anatomy.

"Um, Is It Really a Boy?"

It is important not to confuse sex assigned at birth with gender identity. Where sex assigned at birth is a determination based on external anatomy, gender identity is determined by way of self-identification. Many argue that while sex assigned at birth is a physiological phenomenon, gender identity is a psychological phenomenon. So, where sex assigned at birth can be reduced to whether you look like a boy, a girl, or an intersex person based on your genitalia, gender identity can be reduced to what you feel like or whether you know yourself to be a boy, a girl, both, or neither.

Cisgender versus Transgender

So now that we have a basic understanding of the difference between sex assigned at birth and gender identity, we can begin to discuss the difference between cisgender and transgender identification. When a person is cisgender their sex assigned at birth and their gender identity align in a way consistent with the larger culture's expectations. For example, a cisgender individual would be a person whose sex assigned at birth was male and who identified, in terms of gender, as a boy or a man. Conversely, transgender refers to a person whose sex assigned at birth and gender identity do not align in a manner consistent with cultural expectations. For example, this could be a person whose sex assigned at birth is female but whose gender identity is male. It is important to note that there are also individuals who do not identify exclusively as male or female. This can present itself in a number of ways. For example, a person may identify as a combination of both male and female; they may feel as though they are neither male nor female but instead a third gender; they may also experience the absence of gender. In each of these instances the individual may be considered what we call nonbinary. Nonbinary people are considered by many to be transgender because while their gender identity may not be exclusively male or female, their sex assigned at birth (in most instances) is in fact exclusively male or female. So, when considering our earlier definition of transgender (a person whose sex assigned at birth and gender identity do not align in a manner consistent with cultural expectations), a nonbinary person would fall into that category. Having said that, not all nonbinary individuals identify as transgender, though they certainly could if based solely on the above definition.

When referring to gender identity, we are referring to a profoundly personal construct. An individual's gender identity is known on an intimate level. As such, cisgender, transgender, and nonbinary identification are a matter of self-identification. Knowing this will help you better understand the transgender community.

The Numbers

There are many transgender individuals in the United States. Estimates range from 1.3 million to 2 million transgender adults in the United States alone. Additionally, an estimated 300,000 youth ages 13 to 17 in the United States identify as transgender. While the transgender community is not a monolith, there is some data to speak to common or shared experiences within the community. This chapter will highlight those areas of commonality. It is important to note that data referenced in this chapter will focus on transgender individuals in the United States.

In 2015, the results of the United States Transgender Survey were published. The U.S. Trans Survey focused specifically on the transgender community. What was so interesting about this study, aside from its point of focus, was the sample size. The 2015 U.S. Trans Survey was the largest of its kind. It has been nearly a decade since this study was published, yet despite the lapse in time it remains one of the most informative pieces of literature related to the transgender community. With participation from nearly 28,000 transgender individuals, age 18 and older, this study serves as our best shot at understanding the demographic breakdown of the transgender community in the United States. The rest of this chapter will explore the results of this study, sometimes also supported by U.S. Census numbers.

Our Race

Regarding race, 62.2% identified as White, 16.6% identified as Latino or Latina, 12.6% identified as Black, 5.1%

identified as Asian, 2.5% identified as multiracial, 0.7% identified as American Indian, and 0.4% identified as Middle Eastern. (Because I'm representing the specific categories that the U.S. Census and Trans Survey provide in their forms, I'm using the term "American Indian" as opposed to "Native American" in this chapter.) These numbers are not too far off from the racial demographic information made available by the 2020 U.S. Census which recorded the following: 59.3% identified as White, 18.9% identified as Hispanic or Latino, 13.6% identified as Black, 6.1% identified as Asian, 2.9% identified as two or more races, and 1.3% identified as American Indian and Alaska Native. Unfortunately, the 2020 United States Census did not clearly differentiate those who were from the Middle East or North Africa from those who were White, resulting in our inability to draw a direct comparison between the level of representation of Middle Eastern people in the transgender community as opposed to the general population.

Our Age

When considering the age of respondents, there were some discrepancies between what we know to be the demographic breakdown of age in the United States and the demographic breakdown of the age of individuals who identify as transgender. Some of these discrepancies are worthy of further discussion. According to the census data available at the time of the 2015 U.S. Trans Survey, approximately 13% of individuals in the United States identified between the ages of 18 and 24; however, as it relates to the study, which focused on transgender individuals, 42% of participants identified between the ages of 18 to 24. Stated differently, while only 13% of the U.S. population are between 18 and 24, 42% of those identifying as transgender are between 18 and 24. Additionally, when looking at the age range of 25 to 44, we find that approximately 34% of individuals in the U.S. population fall between the age range of 25 to 44, whereas of those surveyed, 42% were between the ages of 25 to 44. Interestingly, whereas 34% of the U.S. population is between the ages of 46 and 64, only 14% of those surveyed fell between those ages. Lastly, where 19% of the U.S. population is 65 and over, only 2% of those identified as transgender are 65 and over.

So what does all of this mean? It means that transgender identification is heavily skewed toward those who are younger. There may be several reasons that is the case. For one, the survey was conducted online, and because of that, members of the older generation may not have participated as much as those of younger generations. Additionally, societal expectations could be at play because whereas transgender identification was rarely discussed and widely rebuked in times past, some might say that it has become more widely accepted. Can people identify as transgender at a younger age and then stop identifying as transgender as they age? I suppose that's a possibility, but I think that it's less plausible than the likelihood that older individuals are less apt to be open about their transgender identity because they came of age during a time when being transgender was highly scrutinized and potentially dangerous to share with others.

Where We Live

Next, we will discuss the regional representation of transgender identity within the United States. The U.S. transgender survey found interesting results in relation to where in the country transgender individuals are most likely to live. Again we'll compare census information with the survey results to see if there are noteworthy differences between how the country is split up demographically in terms of regions versus how individuals who identify as transgender are split up demographically in terms of regions.

First, we will discuss the Northeast. According to the census data available at the time of the U.S. Trans Survey, 18% of individuals in the United States live in the northeast. Similarly, the survey found that of individuals who identify as transgender, 20% live in the northeast. Next, we will discuss the South. According to the U.S. Census, 38% of individuals in the United States live in the South. The findings in the transgender community are significantly different in that only 29% of those identifying as transgender live in the South. This finding is not surprising in that the South historically has not been viewed as an affirming place for LGBTQ+ individuals. Next, we will discuss the Midwest. According to the U.S. Census, 21% of individuals in the United States live in the Midwest, and that's relatively close to the representation in the transgender community, which has 19% of those who identify as transgender living in the Midwest. Lastly, we will discuss the West. According to the U.S. Census, approximately 24% of individuals in the United States live in the West. The number is higher still for members of the transgender community in that 31% of members of the transgender community live in the West.

Is it a coincidence that areas historically known to be more accepting and affirming of LGBTQ+ individuals are also where transgender individuals are most likely to live? No, that is far from a coincidence. Transgender individuals are more likely to live in the West than they are to live in the South, and that comes as a surprise to no one. Similarly, transgender individuals in less supportive communities might feel less comfortable identifying themselves, even in a survey (anonymous or otherwise). It's also important to keep in mind that each of these geographic regions is diverse, with a range of communities and populations, so the distribution of transgender individuals within them is more nuanced than these numbers can show.

What Language We Speak

Regarding the language spoken in the home, 84% of members of the transgender community reported that English was the only language spoken in their home, which is higher than the 79% of the United States population that reports English being the only language spoken in their home. This finding may or may not be of consequence, but in an attempt to present as comprehensive a picture as possible, I've added this information.

Our Religion, Spirituality, or Lack Thereof

Regarding religion or spirituality, 63% of members of the transgender community report having some connection to religion or spirituality, whereas 37% of members of the transgender community deny having a religious or spiritual identity. What's more, 25% of members of the transgender community identify as being spiritual but not having a religious affiliation. While 21% of transgender individuals identify as Christian, a more significant majority, roughly 45% of transgender individuals, identify as either agnostic or atheist. We'll look at religion again in the "Faith Communities" section later in this chapter.

Our Level of Education

As a transgender man with a PhD in health psychology with a clinical specialization, I find myself particularly interested in the educational attainment of members of the transgender community. The findings of the U.S. Trans Survey related to educational attainment are quite interesting. In short, the results support an understanding that the transgender community, in general, is more educated than the general population. In the general population, 14% have not completed high school. Regarding the transgender community, that number is significantly lower at 3%. In the general population, 30% have only gone as far as completing their high school diploma or GED. The transgender population is half that at 15%. In the general population, 46% have completed some college, either having received an associate's degree or completed some college without obtaining a degree. The transgender community is significantly higher at 65%. In the general population 10% have a bachelor's degree or higher. Regarding the transgender population, the number is considerably higher at 17%. These numbers indicate that members of the transgender community are more likely to attend and complete college than the general population, and they are less likely to stop their education at the level of high school completion or less; this becomes particularly significant when we begin to look at the next section, which discusses economic standing.

Our Finances

In a manner seemingly inconsistent with the previously discussed levels of educational attainment, members of the transgender community are three times more likely to be unemployed than members of the general population. Stated differently, 15% of transgender individuals are unemployed, whereas 5% of the general population are in that position. Similarly, nearly 30% of transgender individuals live in poverty, whereas only 12% of the U.S. population live in poverty.

How is it the case that more-educated individuals are also more likely to live in poverty? How is it that more-educated individuals are more likely to be unemployed? Let's look more closely at the numbers. When we look at income level, what we find is that 1% of members of the general population have no income at all, whereas 4% of the transgender population have no income. In the general population, 4% have an income between $1.00 and $9,999 per year, whereas 12% of the transgender population have that same income level. In the general population, 12% have an income between $10,000 and $24,999 annually, whereas 22% of the transgender population have that income level. In the general population, 21% have an income level of $25,000 to $49,999 per year, whereas 24% of transgender individuals have that same level of income. In the general population, 31% have an income between $50,000 and $99,999 yearly, whereas only 23% of the transgender population have that income. And lastly, 31% of the general population have an income of $100,000 or more a year, whereas only 15% of transgender individuals have an income of over $100,000 a year.

Members of the transgender community are more likely to live in poverty and to be unemployed than members of the general population despite having higher levels of education. One would be hard-pressed to explain this phenomenon without explicitly pointing to discrimination, lack of access and opportunity, and overt and covert bias as contributing factors.

Our Disabilities

Regarding disabilities, 39% of the transgender community identify as having one or more disabilities, whereas only 15% of the general population identify as having one or more disabilities. While being deaf or having serious difficulty hearing, being blind or having serious difficulty seeing even when wearing eyeglasses, and having serious difficulty walking or climbing stairs were relatively similar in both the transgender population and the general population, some items were significantly different. For example, when it came to having difficulty concentrating, remembering, or making decisions because of a physical, mental, or emotional condition, 30% of transgender individuals reported having this experience versus 5% of the general population. Similarly, when it came to having difficulty doing errands alone because of a physical, mental, or emotional condition, 22% of transgender individuals reported this difficulty, as opposed to 6% of the general population.

Our Citizenship

Transgender individuals are more likely to be citizens by birth than the general population. Ninety-four percent of transgender individuals are citizens by birth, and another 3% are naturalized citizens, compared to 16% of members of the general population who are not citizens by birth.

Our Sexual Orientation

Sexual orientation and gender identity are not the same. Sexual orientation is who you are attracted to, and this attraction can be sexual, physical, emotional, spiritual, aesthetic, or otherwise. Gender identity is who you know yourself to be. Gender identity focuses on the construct of gender, meaning whether you identify as a man, a woman, both, or neither. And while both sexual orientation and gender identity are nuanced and complex, it is essential that you not confuse the two. People often make assumptions about a person's sexual orientation that are based solely on their gender identity. For example, one might assume that a transgender woman will automatically be attracted to men, but that is not necessarily the case. The reality is that a person can have any combination of sexual orientation and gender identity.

Now, let's look at sexual orientation in the transgender community more closely. Among the transgender community,

21% identify as queer (an umbrella term utilized to signify that a person does not identify in a manner consistent with assumptions of cisgender and/or heterosexual identification); 18% identify as pansexual (which is the ability to be attracted to individuals of any gender identity); 16% identify as gay, lesbian, or same-gender loving; 15% identify as straight; 14% identify as bisexual; and 10% identify as asexual. These numbers quickly highlight why assumptions regarding sexual orientation based on gender identity are often inaccurate. If we were to utilize the previous example of assuming that a transgender woman must be exclusively attracted to men, which is to assume that she must be straight, we would find that assumption may be wrong 85% of the time because only 15% of transgender individuals identify as straight.

Our Marriage Status

Members of the general population are more likely than members of the transgender community to be married. This finding is consistent no matter the age. Between ages 18 and 24, 8% of the general population report being married, whereas only 3% of the transgender community report the same. Between the ages of 25 and 44, 53% of the general population report being married, whereas only 23% of the transgender community report the same. Between ages 45 and 64, 66% of the general population report being married, whereas only 42% of the transgender community report marriage. Lastly, among those 65 and over, 56% of the general population report being married, whereas only 45% of the transgender community report being married.

Being "Out" in Intimate Relationships

The U.S. Trans Survey also looked into the extent to which members of the transgender community were "out" about their transgender identity, meaning that they'd revealed their identity to someone. As we review these findings, we'll start with the most intimate relationships. Among members of the transgender community, 86% report having either a current spouse or partner or a former spouse or partner. Interestingly, 58% were out to their current spouse or partner, while 53% had been out to at least one of their previous spouses or partners. The study found that overall, 88% of transgender individuals are either currently out to their current spouse or partner or had been out to a former spouse or partner.

The Consequences of Being Out

Being out, however, is not without consequences. Unfortunately, some members of the transgender community have lost spouses or partners due to coming out as transgender. Among the transgender community, 27% reported that a partner ended their relationship either solely or partly because they were transgender, and 10% said that a partner or spouse ended their relationship solely because they were transgender.

The likelihood of this occurring varied with age. The older an individual is (currently), the more likely a spouse or partner ended the relationship solely because they were transgender. While 6% of transgender individuals between the ages of 18 to 24 had a spouse or partner end their relationship solely because they were transgender, the percentage for those 65 and over was 20%.

A transgender person's current age was not the only thing that appeared to impact the likelihood of their spouse or partner leaving them because they were transgender. It was also the case that the age at which the transgender person transitioned also impacted whether their relationship ended solely because of their transgender identity. Those under the age of 18 only experienced this 12% of the time and those 35 and over experienced it twice the rate at 24% of the time.

Gender identity also appears to play a role in whether a relationship is ended solely based on a person identifying as transgender, with 18% of transgender women reporting that a spouse or partner ended their relationship with them solely because of their being transgender, which is twice the rate of transgender men, who report experiencing this 9% of the time, and six times the rate of nonbinary individuals, who report experiencing this only 3% of the time.

Our Relationships with Our Children

Another significant relationship to consider is that between a transgender person and their children. The U.S. Trans Survey found that 18% of individuals in the transgender community are, in fact, parents; of those who are parents, 69% are out as transgender to at least one of their children. Being a parent and having your children living in the home with you, however, are two different things. The survey found that while 34% of adults in the U.S. population have at least one related child under 18 living with them, the number was far less for members of the transgender community, where the number was only 14%. This finding was most striking for members of the transgender community between the ages of 25 and 44. The survey found that 54% of members of the general population in that age group have children under 18 who are related to them living with them. Only 12% of the transgender community between the ages of 25 and 44 have related children living with them.

The survey revealed another aspect of parents' relationships with their children. Sadly, 21% of transgender individuals who were out to their children reported that at least one of their children either stopped talking to them or stopped spending time with them temporarily or permanently due to their transgender identity. This finding impacted the relationship of trans women and their children more than any other subgroup, with 28% of transgender women with children reporting that at least one of their children stopped spending time with or talking to them either temporarily or permanently because they were transgender. This number was much lower for transgender men and individuals who identify as nonbinary. Among both subgroups, 6% reported that their children either stopped talking to or spending time with them after learning they were transgender.

Our Immediate Family

Now let's widen the lens beyond focusing specifically on spouses, partners, and children to look at the immediate family more broadly. Among the transgender community, 26% of individuals who are out to their immediate family reported that at least one family member either stopped speaking to them or ended the relationship with them altogether. Worse still, 10% of transgender individuals report that they experienced violence toward them by a family member. Other hardships include 8% being kicked out of the house, 14% being sent to a professional so that they could somehow be made to no longer be transgender, and 27% not being able to wear clothes that match their gender identity. For these and other reasons, 10% run away from home, and of those who run away from home, 32% of them run away at age 15 or younger.

Being Kicked Out

As noted in the previous section, 8% of members of the transgender community who are out to their family are kicked out of the house because they are transgender. People of color are the most likely to be kicked out of their homes for being transgender. Of those kicked out of their home, 17% identified as Middle Eastern, 14% American Indian, 12% Black, 11% Latino or Latina, 11% multiracial, 9% Asian, and 6% White.

Unfortunately, being kicked out of the house is associated with several detrimental outcomes, and the long-term impacts should not be ignored. Transgender individuals who are kicked out of the house are more likely to live in poverty and have lower incomes overall. They are three times more likely to have engaged in sex work, and 74% experienced homelessness. They are more than twice as likely to be living with HIV, are at significant risk of attempting suicide, and have an increased risk of experiencing psychological distress. All in all, 50% of those in the transgender community who are out to their family as transgender experience some form of rejection by their family.

Supportive Family

The good news is that not all members of the transgender community who are out to their family experience violence or rejection; 82% of them report having experienced some level of support from at least one family member. So how does this support look? Well, 65% reported that they had a family member tell them that they support them or respect them; 58% reported a family member used their chosen name; 55% reported a family member used the correct pronouns; 36% reported a family member stood up for them; 33% reported a family member did research to try to learn how to support them best; 18% reported that a family member gave money to help in their transition; 11% reported that a family member supported them in some other way; and 10% reported that a family member provided them help with changing their name and/or gender on ID documents. The impact of such support cannot be overstated.

Faith Communities

Faith communities can play an essential role in the lives of members of the transgender community. This notion is supported by the fact that the U.S. Trans survey found that

66% of members of the transgender community report that they have been part of a faith community at some point in their life. This number is highest in the Black community, with 77% of Black transgender individuals reporting having been a part of a faith community at some point in their life, followed by members of the Middle Eastern community at 71%. Numbers are relatively high for the other communities as well, with 66% of White transgender individuals reporting having been a part of a faith community at some point in their life, followed closely by 65% of those who identify as American Indian or multiracial, 62% of those who identify as Latino or Latina, and 59% of those who identify as Asian.

Unfortunately, despite this initial connection, members of the transgender community aren't always able to stay involved with their faith communities. They often leave their faith communities due to either fearing rejection or experiencing rejection. It's important to note that 39% of members of the transgender community left communities of faith for fear of rejection, whereas 19% left due to experiencing rejection. These experiences, like others, differ with race and ethnicity. For example, 54% of Middle Eastern individuals identifying as transgender left a faith community due to fear of rejection, as opposed to 35% of their White counterparts. Likewise, 33% of American Indians who identify as transgender left their faith community due to experiencing rejection, as opposed to 17% of their White counterparts. However, all is not lost. Of those who experienced rejection by their faith communities, 42% found a new community that welcomed them.

Overall Health

When given the opportunity to rate their overall health, members of the transgender community rate their health in a manner relatively similar to members of the general population. However, two areas show a difference worth noting: rating one's overall health as fair and rating one's overall health as excellent. Members of the transgender community rate their overall health as fair 17% of the time, and members of the general population rate their overall health as fair 13% of the time. Conversely, when rating their overall health as excellent, members of the transgender community only rate their overall health as excellent 12% of the time, whereas members of the general population rate their overall health as excellent 19% of the time.

Mental Health

As it relates to mental health, the U.S. Trans Survey looked at levels of psychological distress, in particular, if the levels were so significant that they interfered with the individual's life or activities. Members of the transgender community who reported experiencing significant psychological distress were able to say that distress did not impact their life or activities at all 10% of the time. This finding is interesting, and at first glance you might look at it as a testament to resilience, and perhaps it is. But it's important to note that in the general population, those who report experiencing significant psychological distress are able to say that distress does not impact their life or activities 35% of the time. Similarly, and in a manner that I find to be just as concerning, while only 12% of members of the general population who report experiencing significant psychological distress state that the distress impacts their life or their activities a lot of the time, that percentage is significantly higher with members of the transgender community, who report that their experience of significant psychological distress impacts their life or activities a lot 29% of the time. This finding is even more concerning when you consider what percentage of transgender individuals are currently experiencing serious psychological distress. The survey indicates that 39% of transgender individuals report currently experiencing serious psychological distress, which is significantly higher than the 5% of the general population that reports the same.

I would be remiss if I discussed psychological distress in the transgender community without discussing suicidality expressly. Suicidality is a problem in the transgender community. The statistics around suicidal ideations and suicide attempts are alarming. Transgender individuals are nearly 10 times more likely than members of the general population to attempt suicide at some point; 4.6% of members of the general population have attempted suicide at some point in their life, whereas 40% of members of the transgender community have attempted suicide at some point in their life. As it relates to suicidal ideation, 4% of the general population in the United States has seriously thought about dying by suicide in the past year, whereas 48% of members of the transgender community in the United States have thought the same. Among members of the general population, 1.1% have devised a plan to die by suicide in the past year, compared to 24% of members of the transgender community. While 0.6% of the U.S. population has attempted suicide in the past year, that number is 7% among members of the transgender community. Sadly, suicide is often attempted more than once; 71% of members of the transgender community report having attempted suicide on more than one occasion in their lifetime. Just as alarming is that 46% of those who have attempted suicide in the transgender community report doing so three or more times.

Detransitioning

Detransitioning is when a member of the transgender community goes back to living as the sex they were assigned at birth. The fact that some individuals detransition is often weaponized by individuals who do not support the transgender community and is used as a means to convince people that regret is a common occurrence among those who detransition, which simply is not the case. The U.S. Trans Survey found that only 8% of individuals in the transgender community reported detransitioning. Of that 8%, the majority only detransitioned temporarily, with more than 60% ultimately going on to live their lives in a manner consistent with their gender identity as opposed to the sex they were assigned at birth.

It's important to understand why people detransition, however, and the survey found that there were multiple reasons for engaging in this behavior, whether temporarily or permanently. Among individuals who detransition (even if just temporarily), 36% reported that they did so as a result of pressure from a parent; 33% reported that they detransitioned because transitioning was too hard for them; 31% reported that they detransitioned because they faced too much harassment or discrimination as a transgender person; 29% reported that they detransitioned because they had trouble getting a job; 26% reported that they detransitioned because of pressure from other family members; 18% reported that they detransitioned because of pressure from a spouse or partner; 17% reported that they detransitioned because of pressure from an employer; 13% reported that they detransitioned because of pressure from their friends; 5% reported that they detransitioned because of pressure from a mental health professional; 5% reported that they detransitioned because of pressure from a religious counselor; 5% reported that they detransitioned because they realized that gender transition was not for them; 4% reported that they detransitioned because the initial transition did not reflect the complexity of their gender identity; 3% reported that they detransitioned for financial reasons; 2% reported that they detransitioned for medical reasons; and 35% reported that they detransitioned for reasons not listed above. So not only is it rare that individuals of the transgender community engage in detransitioning, but when they do, the reasons for that decision are complex, nuanced, and often the direct result of societal pressure.

Not Homogenous

Is this the complete picture? No. I don't know how one presents the full picture as it relates to any group of people. In fact, presenting the complete picture is not even the goal. The goal is to highlight that transgender individuals are whole persons. They should not be reduced to their gender identity or expression but should be recognized and celebrated in their fullness. The purpose of this chapter is to make clear that transgender people are not homogeneous. They are beautiful. They are vibrant. They are nuanced. And while the comprehensive understanding of this community is beyond the scope of this chapter and even this book, this information serves as a great starting point for those who care to know more about this community. If you are a cisgender person, hopefully you can see that your transgender counterparts are both very much like you and simultaneously not like you at all.

Just as most adults spend a significant portion of their waking hours at work, so do transgender individuals, so it is essential that we understand what their experiences are like in the workplace. And that is precisely what we will discuss in the next chapter.

Chapter 2

Experiences in the Workplace

Being lesbian, gay, or bisexual in the workplace is hard. Being transgender in the workplace can be even harder.

Data shows that transgender individuals often experience maltreatment in the workplace. Many aspects of the work experience are impacted, from hiring to firing and everything in between. Often, the ability to respond to or avoid discrimination is limited. So it comes as no surprise that many individuals are not out as transgender in the workplace.

Being Out in the Workplace

According to the U.S. Trans Survey, 49% of transgender individuals currently working report that they are not out as transgender to any of their bosses or supervisors. It took me many years to come out as transgender to a supervisor or boss. I was afraid of the possible ramifications. I had been working so hard to prove myself and my efforts had gotten the attention of those above me. I knew that I was a rising star in the organization but I worried all of that would come crumbling down around me if my superiors found out that I was transgender. So I hid it. I hid it until I felt I had proven my worth so much so that I had some job security. And I hid it until I had a boss whom I believed genuinely cared for me and my well-being. Even then I was afraid. What if I had misjudged my boss and their level of acceptance? I had a family to take care of and I found myself grappling with whether I should come out as transgender and remove what had become a heavy burden from my shoulders or whether I should continue to carry that burden in an attempt to make sure that I maintained my ability to take care of my family. I spent the next 18 months being misgendered and deadnamed. No one knew any differently. I prioritized my ability to take care of my family and became increasingly miserable as time passed. Again, it wasn't until I left that facility and I had a new boss that I came out as transgender.

And this phenomenon is not limited to interactions with people in positions of authority; 42% of transgender employees report that none of their coworkers know they are transgender. Of those who are out as transgender to their coworkers, 68% say that their coworkers are very supportive of them, 29% report that they have coworkers who are neither supportive nor unsupportive, and 3% have unsupportive coworkers. One might look at that statistic and think that the workplace is a safe environment for a transgender person. But this statistic may be more a testament to the ability of transgender individuals to discern who is safe to out themselves to, rather than a testament to how safe work environments are for members of the transgender community. It also doesn't take into account coworkers who are outwardly supportive but might not truly be as supportive under the surface (whether consciously or subconsciously). In my case I was in a position of authority. I walked in a certain amount of privilege. Even if people had a problem with my gender identity, they were not likely to mention it to me, as a member of the executive team. But not everyone has that privilege, and if I was afraid, despite my positioning, I can only imagine what others might be experiencing.

Being able to ascertain whether someone is safe to out yourself to is essential for transgender individuals. But this requires that you get to know someone. What if you're not provided with an opportunity to get to know a person? That makes it more difficult to gauge whether being out as transgender is safe. This can be even harder in situations where people work remotely. In that instance you might find that you have very limited opportunities to share that aspect of your life with people and that some of the ways that people share without verbalizing (such as grooming and clothing) are not as easily noticed by your peers when you work remotely, possibly making the introduction of the topic more challenging. Another concern is that a person may know that they are safe within their own company or organization but this is no guarantee that they are safe in the presence of other organizations, customers, suppliers, or the general public. Perhaps these reasons contribute to why, according to McKinsey & Company, 66% of transgender employees report not being out in professional interactions outside their own companies.

Discrimination in Hiring, Promoting, and Firing

The U.S. Trans Survey looked at three instances of discrimination: not being hired for a job you've applied for, being denied a promotion, and being fired or forced to resign. When asked about their experiences over the past year, 67% of transgender individuals who held or applied for a job reported that they were not hired or promoted or were fired or forced to resign. Not all of these individuals attribute this experience to gender identity or expression.

However, 39% of those who experienced not being hired in the past year report that they were not hired because of their gender identity or expression; 49% reported that their gender identity or expression was the reason they were not promoted; and 43% report that their gender identity or expression was the reason they were terminated or made to resign.

These statistics really hit close to home for me. I remember applying for jobs and running into what I painfully call the "pink and blue ceiling." I would apply to jobs and would go through round after round of interviews. I would interview exceptionally well and the hiring manager would tell me how much they thought I would be an asset to the team, and then something strange would happen. Once I shared that I was transgender the communication would stop, the interest would wane, and the verbal offers would not materialize into written offers. This happened over and over and over again. And then one day, someone finally said the quiet part out loud. A hiring manager shared with me that they wanted to hire me and that they had tried to do so, but that they were stopped by their boss because I was transgender. I'll never forget that conversation. You could hear the disappointment in his voice. He said, "I really want to work with you. I think you would be great, it's just that, well the big bosses are kind of conservative and they just won't allow it." I was crushed. It wasn't many months later that a recruiter shared a similar sentiment with me. He had been trying to place me in a CEO role for a freestanding psychiatric facility. He and I had worked together for months. He had presented me to several organizations to no avail. He was honest with me about the fact that with my experience and pedigree I should have been placed easily. After a few months of trying, he gave up. The reason I wasn't being selected was a reason that was not going to change. I was transgender and there didn't seem to be a way to get around that. Eventually, he just stopped calling.

Response to Discrimination in the Workplace

One might wonder how transgender individuals respond to negative experiences in the workplace. It's challenging to accurately assess responses to the various forms of mistreatment that transgender individuals experience. However, the U.S. Trans Survey asked how transgender individuals responded when they were fired due to their gender identity or expression, and the findings are striking: 69% of transgender individuals who report having been fired or forced to resign due to their gender identity or expression did not do anything in response to having had that experience. Stated differently, nearly 70% of transgender individuals who were wrongfully fired or forced to resign because of their gender identity or expression accepted the termination without fighting back; 15% contacted a lawyer; 14% made an official complaint; 10% contacted a transgender-specific, LGBTQ+, or other group; 2% contacted their union representative. And 7% responded in a way not specified above.

So even though individuals know that they are being discriminated against and being fired or forced to resign because they are transgender, the lion's share of them accept the wrongful termination or forced resignation without pushing back. It's not hard to guess why this would be the case. Some of the reasons include feeling defeated, believing nothing will come of their efforts, not knowing what their options are, and fearing retaliation. And sometimes the very people in the workplace to whom they need to report the discrimination are also known to engage in discriminatory behavior. Sadly, no discipline is immune to bias and discriminatory behavior, and human resources is no exception.

This brings to mind a situation in which I was denied a promotion due to being transgender. I contacted a lawyer, who advised that I had a very clear case of discrimination but warned me that pursuing a legal remedy could result in me being blacklisted by this company and as a part of the settlement I would probably be required never to work with or for them again in the future. I wrestled with the decision, particularly because it was one of the largest organizations in my industry and being blacklisted by them would quite literally remove nearly half my employment opportunities in the nation. As hurt as I was by their refusal to promote me because I was transgender, I was scared that I would be unable to take care of my family if I rocked the boat. So I didn't pursue legal action. I regret that decision to this day. Less than a year later, I was pushed out for "budgetary reasons." They had no concerns about my performance or work record. They just decided to get rid of my position. And that was it. I was out of a job and I had no recourse.

As previously stated, only 14% of individuals who were wrongfully terminated or forced to resign because of their gender identity file an official complaint. Of those who do so, here's where they file it:

- 53% file it with their employer's human resources or personnel department.
- 33% file a complaint with the Equal Employment Opportunity Commission.
- 18% file a complaint with the employer's Equal Employment Opportunity office.
- 17% file a complaint with the local or state Human Rights Commission.
- 9% file a complaint with their supervisor or manager.
- 26% file a complaint in a manner not listed above.

Why does this matter? Because it shows us that an individual who is wrongfully terminated or forced to resign because of their gender identity is not likely to file an official complaint. That means we are likely to be unaware when such discriminatory behavior occurs. So if we want to intervene in a meaningful way and protect individuals from these experiences, we have to be proactive and get in front of the discriminatory behavior before it happens. We must be purposeful in the creation (or revision) of our policies and procedures. We must make certain that individuals have a mechanism by which to make it known if they are experiencing discrimination or bullying and then we must ensure that our response to such allegations is swift and thorough.

What's more, 53% of the individuals who officially report this behavior will report it to their employer's human resources department. That might initially sound like an encouraging number, but it also means that nearly 50% of the people don't feel that going to their employer's human resources department is the right move. There can be several reasons for this. Sometimes a broad culture of transphobia permeates every aspect of the workplace, including human resources. At other times the human resources department might be known to have failed to support individuals who have brought official complaints in the past. And sometimes specific human resource personnel might have behaved in a way that causes transgender individuals to question the safety of disclosing their experience to them. In my case, I notified human resources and found that they very quickly closed ranks and immediately began to maneuver in a manner meant to protect the organization. If I were to experience this again, I might not notify human resources because in my experience their rallying cry was very clearly the protection of the company. There can be many reasons a person does not notify human resources of their maltreatment. Whatever the reason, we should be concerned. Many organizations rely heavily on the human resources function to receive complaints of maltreatment and have no other means of tracking problematic behavior; these statistics highlight the inherent risk in that approach.

As previously mentioned, 15% of individuals fired or forced to resign because of their gender identity contact a lawyer. Of those who do, they report the following experiences:

- 29% found that they were not able to hire the lawyer.
- 21% reported that the lawyer filed a lawsuit.

- 14% said that the lawyer helped them to file an official complaint.

- 10% reported that the lawyer called or wrote a letter to the employer.

- 10% stated that the lawyer advised them to take no action.

- 7% reported that the lawyer did nothing or did not follow up.

- 9% said the lawyer responded in a way not listed above.

These statistics are important because they make us aware that we cannot rely upon legal filings and the frequency with which they occur to assess the extent to which we have a problem in the area of the wrongful termination or forced resignation of transgender individuals. If we rely solely on litigation data, we overlook the real-world experiences of many individuals.

Other Forms of Workplace Discrimination

Being fired, not being hired, and not being promoted are not the only ways a person can experience discrimination in the workplace. Transgender individuals report other forms of discrimination as well: 16% report that someone in the workplace shared personal information about them that should not have been shared; 6% report that they received a negative review from their boss because they were transgender; 4% were instructed to present themselves in a manner inconsistent with their gender identity to keep their job. And 4% said they were not allowed to use the restroom that was consistent with their gender identity. Also, 3% reported that their employer or boss removed them from direct contact with clients, customers, or patients. And 2% reported that their employer or boss forced them to transfer to a different position or department.

Attempts to Avoid Discrimination

With discrimination being so prevalent, it's no wonder that transgender individuals engage in behaviors or take actions to avoid anti-transgender discrimination in the workplace. When asked what actions they took to avoid discrimination in the past year, transgender employees reported that 53% hid their gender identity; 47% did not ask their employer to use the appropriate pronouns; 26% delayed their gender transition; 26% stayed in a job that they would have preferred to leave; 25% hid that they had already transitioned their gender; 24% kept a job for which they were overqualified; 15% quit their job; 30% did not seek a promotion or a raise; 6% requested or transferred to a different position or department. And 77% reported that they engaged in one or more of the previously discussed behaviors to avoid anti-transgender discrimination.

Some individuals were more likely than others to engage in these active attempts to avoid anti-transgender discrimination. Those who were living in poverty, those who identified as nonbinary, and those with disabilities were actually at an increased likelihood of engaging in behaviors to avoid anti-transgender discrimination. This may be because they felt that they were at increased risk.

Seeking Employment

According to a survey published by McKinsey & Company in 2021, transgender individuals often experience challenges in the actual job-seeking process. They found that 50% of transgender individuals reported that they could not be their full, authentic selves during the interview process. I often get asked if a person should disclose that they are transgender during the interview process, and the truth of the matter is that there is no easy answer. Sometimes I hear people say things like, "You should tell them so that they can avoid hiring you if they have a problem with you being transgender." They normally give this advice under the guise of protecting you from ending up working in a toxic environment. But I worry that advice is only truly accessible to individuals who can afford not to be selected for employment time and time again. If you are already employed or have the means to go without employment for a time, that advice might be OK, but if you need to work to care for yourself and your loved ones, you may not be able to afford to miss out on multiple opportunities, no matter the reason.

Limited Advancement Opportunities

Additionally, research suggests that there are limitations placed on the career advancement of transgender individuals. McKinsey & Company found that transgender individuals were more likely than cisgender individuals to be entry-level employees, were similarly positioned in their likelihood to be in non-manager positions above entry-level, and were significantly less likely to be a manager or a senior leader. And what is the impact of this pink and blue ceiling? One fairly obvious result is that you don't have many transgender individuals in management or senior-level positions. But what is potentially overlooked is that the absence of transgender individuals in those roles equates to the absence of transgender role models. Suppose you are more likely to be an entry-level employee and less likely to be a manager or a senior leader. In that case, you are likely to be in a position where you are looking up, and sadly, you're not likely to see anyone who looks like you.

Speaking of seeing someone who looks like you, there is a significant portion of the transgender experience that centers around our ability to see someone who looks like us – not just people who look like us outside of ourselves but seeing someone who looks like us when we look at ourselves. It is this desire to be who we know ourselves to be that can lead to many of us choosing to transition socially, legally, and/or medically. We will discuss the process of transition in the next chapter.

Part II

Core Questions About Transition

Chapter 3

A Basic Understanding of Transition

Many transgender individuals desire to transition. Sadly, not all of us are able.

There are three widely recognized forms of transition in the transgender community: medical, legal, and social transition. A person may transition in none, some, or all ways. Transition is not a prerequisite for membership in the transgender community. There are many reasons a person may not transition or may only transition in some ways but not others (finances, access, safety, physical limitations, or desire, to name a few). You are not any less transgender if you do not transition. It is imperative that transitioning not be used as a means of gatekeeping the transgender community. But it is important to understand social, medical, and legal transitioning.

Social Transition

Social transition is the most readily available and, likewise, the most widely accessible. Social transition has everything to do with how you show up in the world. It is how you dress, your chosen name, and your chosen pronouns; it is how you relate to the world and how you express your gender to those around you. Gender is a social construct, and we are socialized to view certain things through a specific gender lens. For example, certain clothing items, career paths, and names are socialized to specific genders.

While social transition is the most common form of transition, not all individuals transition in this way. There are several reasons for this. A person simply might not want to transition socially, which is entirely valid. A person might desire to transition socially but might not have the means. For example, purchasing a completely new wardrobe may be cost-prohibitive for an individual. A person may wish to transition socially but fear the repercussions. So it is not always the case that a transgender person will transition socially, and you should not assume that a person is not transgender if they do not transition socially. There are many examples of social transition. I will share some common examples below.

Deciding Whether to Come Out

Coming out to friends and family as transgender is often one of the first steps people take in the process of social transition. For many individuals, having at least a cursory conversation with them about their gender identity is an essential foundation so they can ask people to honor their newly embraced gender expression. Suppose you're transgender and interacting with people you've never met before. In that case, you might be able to avoid this step altogether, particularly if you can pass as a cisgender person of the gender you know yourself to be. For many people, however, this is not the case, so the first step in engaging with those around you in a manner consistent with your identity is coming out to them as transgender.

It's really important to distinguish between the process or desire to come out as transgender and the process or desire to come out as gay. While coming out as transgender or gay can be difficult and potentially dangerous for both groups, often the desire to come out is different for someone who is gay than it is for someone who is transgender. Often, individuals who are lesbian, gay, bisexual, or pansexual desire to come out and be known as their authentic selves and to be accepted, loved, and affirmed. In that way, coming out can often be viewed as celebratory.

But the transgender experience can be very different in that not all transgender individuals desire for people to know that they're transgender. Instead, they want to transition and to simply be known as the person they have always known themselves to be without reference to, acknowledgment of, or unnecessary revisiting of the gender associated with the sex they were assigned at birth. For this reason, coming out as transgender may not even be a person's desire. Frequently the goal is to be able to pass as cisgender and to have people not experience them as anything other than the gender that aligns with their identity.

While some individuals might distance themselves from the word "transgender" and would prefer to be known simply as a man or a woman, for others being transgender is a significant part of their identity. I'm one of those individuals. You'll rarely hear me refer to myself simply as a man. Instead, you'll likely hear me refer to myself as a transgender man. The transition from female to male is integral to my life's journey and has shaped me in many ways. Because of this, I out myself constantly by introducing myself as a trans man. A great many transgender people do not do this, and that is completely valid, but for me, it is an important distinction.

Requesting the Use of Appropriate Pronouns

Often for members of the transgender community, the gender pronouns that are associated with the sex they were assigned at birth are not an accurate representation of who they know themselves to be. For this reason, they often ask to be referred to with the gender pronouns that are associated with their actual gender identity. Making this request to be referred to with the appropriate pronouns is a form of social transition.

Once a transgender person has made it known what pronouns best represent them, the expectation and the hope is that other people will honor that and will refer to the person as such. When other people refer to the transgender person utilizing pronouns that are different from their chosen pronouns, they are engaging in what is called *misgendering*. Misgendering is potentially harmful and has been associated with increased depression and suicidality for members of the transgender and nonbinary community. When you misgender a person, they can experience significant dysphoria because it communicates to them that you don't see them as the person they know themselves to be. Instead, you see them as someone other than who they are, or perhaps even more damagingly, you don't see them at all.

It's important to be aware that pronouns are not always gendered. There are gendered pronouns like he and his, which are gendered masculinely, or she and her, which are gendered femininely. But you also have what are referred to as gender-neutral pronouns or nonbinary pronouns. The most common nonbinary pronouns for an individual are they and their, although others exist, such as ze and zir.

Requesting the Use of a Different Name

Another form of social transition is when transgender individuals ask people to utilize their chosen name instead of their given name. Often, members of the transgender community select a chosen name to replace their given name. They do this primarily because their given name is highly gendered and, as a result, gives the impression that their gender identity is consistent with the sex they were assigned at birth as opposed to their true gender identity. For example, if a person's given name were Priscilla, individuals would automatically assume that person is a woman. They would immediately begin to refer to them utilizing feminine pronouns such as she, her, and hers. For this reason, having a given name that is highly gendered in the direction of the sex that a transgender person was assigned at birth increases the likelihood that they'll be misgendered. As a result, many transgender individuals select a name that is gendered in a manner that is consistent with their true gender identity.

Similarly, many transgender individuals will select an entirely different name, one that is not clearly gendered in either direction. I'm a perfect example of this. My given name is gendered in such a way that when people see it, they often misgender me and refer to me using she, her, or hers. In order to avoid being misgendered and being seen as a woman when I do not identify as a woman, I stopped utilizing my given name, and I began to request that people refer to me as A.C. A.C. is not my given name; it is my chosen name. But I find that I get misgendered less often by individuals who do not know me if they see the name A.C. written on a piece of paper as opposed to my given name.

A Basic Understanding of Transition

You may have noticed that I've not actually said what my given name is. There's a reason for that. I've not shared my given name because hearing or even seeing my given name causes me to experience significant dysphoria. My given name is associated with years and years of agonizing over my gender identity, being misgendered, being misunderstood, and not being accepted. Consequently, being called by that name is painful to me.

This is not unique to me. Many individuals in the transgender community no longer utilize their given names. They have separated themselves entirely from that name, so much so that the given name is often referred to in the transgender community as the *deadname*. It is the deadname because the person no longer utilizes it, and they desire for it to be gone forever and never to be used again. Their given name is dead to them, as is, for many individuals, the person associated with that name.

So when someone calls a transgender person by their given name as opposed to their chosen name, they are engaging in what is known as *deadnaming*, which is psychologically harmful, can cause significant experiences of dysphoria, and much like misgendering has been linked to increased depression and suicidality in transgender individuals.

Dressing in Alignment with Your Gender Identity

Just like pronouns and names are gendered, so is clothing. We are socialized to believe that certain articles of clothing are most appropriately worn by men and certain articles of clothing are most appropriately worn by women.

For example, skirts, dresses, high heels, and pearls are all items that we have been socialized to associate with the feminine. Conversely, neckties and sports coats are thought to be more appropriately worn by men. This belief system runs so deep that we have entire department stores based on these distinctions, and even when the entire store is not devoted to one gender or the other, often sections within the stores are.

Due to this socialization that associates clothing with gender, often transgender individuals will begin to dress in attire associated with the gender that they know themselves to be as opposed to the gender associated with the sex that they were assigned at birth. Dressing in this way is a form of social transition. I, for example, dress in the men's big and tall section. On any given day, you're likely to see me in a button-down dress shirt, a sweater vest, some dress pants, and a pair of oxfords. I dress in a manner consistent with my gender identity, and I do so on a full-time basis.

Grooming in Ways That Align with Your Gender Identity

Grooming is often a highly gendered act. There are different and often strongly critiqued grooming standards for men and women. Masculine versus feminine grooming is an entire industry. Men have barber shops, and women have beauty salons. Most grooming products such as shampoos, conditioners, body washes, and colognes are often gendered specifically to target men or women. Even items that serve the exact same purpose for both men and women are gendered differently. One example of this is pink-handled razors versus blue-handled razors.

Similarly, we have pink cans of shaving cream that are florally scented versus blue cans of shaving cream that are scented like the outdoors. Some bars of soap are scented in a sweet fragrance and some are scented in an athletic or sports-related fragrance. Likewise, we have perfumes and soothing lotions versus colognes and aftershave. All of these are examples of the grooming industry's recognition of the fact that we've been socialized to view grooming through a gendered lens. Transgender individuals will often groom themselves in a manner consistent with their gender identity instead of the sex they were assigned at birth, and that is a form of social transition.

Creating Body Contour Without Medical Intervention

Sometimes, a transgender individual will change the appearance of their body without undergoing medical intervention. This might be the case for multiple reasons, including lack of desire, lack of means, health concerns, and more. If someone engages in methods to alter the appearance of their body contour that fall short of medical intervention, these actions would fall under the category of social transition. In most instances, the desire is to either create the appearance of or diminish the appearance of secondary sex characteristics. Some examples are discussed in the following sections.

Packing

Packing is the creation of a bulge in your pants or underwear that gives the impression of a penis. Transgender men sometimes engage in packing. There are many ways to pack, including informal and inexpensive ways like placing a sock or a piece of rolled-up fabric in your underwear. There are also more formal and likewise expensive ways, like purchasing a packer, which is essentially a penis prosthetic worn underneath the clothing to give the contour of a penis. Packing is an alternative to surgical intervention such as phalloplasty.

Tucking

Tucking is essentially the opposite of packing. Tucking is when a transgender woman seeks to make the presence of a penis and testicles less noticeable. There are a couple of ways that a person can engage in tucking that range from simply pushing the penis and the testicles back and placing on a tight pair of undergarments so that you're left with a more feminine genital contour, or, in some cases, actually tucking the testicles into the inguinal canal while also pulling the penis back and placing on a tight undergarment. It is important to know that tucking can decrease sperm quantity or quality. This decrease is due to the increased heat the testes experience when placed in the inguinal canal and up close to the body. The purpose of the testicles is to do the exact opposite of that, to create some distance between sperm and the heat of your body, and so when you tuck, you remove that distance and place the sperm directly near the heat source. Tucking is an alternative to surgical interventions such as vaginoplasty or bilateral orchiectomy.

Binding

Transgender men who have not undergone surgical intervention often engage in binding. Binding is when you utilize specially made tape or bandages or specially modified clothing to flatten the appearance of the chest. Binding allows for a more masculine chest contour. It's important when binding not to utilize inexpensive but potentially dangerous methods such as ace bandages or duct tape. Utilizing such items, which are not meant for binding the chest, can cause physical harm because they do not move with the body and they restrict movement in a way that can cause difficulty breathing and, in some instances, broken ribs. Binding is an alternative to top surgery, such as breast reduction or removal.

Padding

Transgender women often engage in padding, which gives the appearance of larger breasts, hips, or buttocks. This can range from wearing padded bras and underwear to wearing breast, hip, and buttocks prostheses. Padding is an alternative to medical interventions such as breast augmentation or injecting silicone into the buttocks.

Medical Transition

While getting exact statistics is difficult for the transgender community, it is estimated that 61% of transgender individuals transition medically, and by that, I mean that they undergo either surgical intervention or hormonal intervention. If you look simply at those who undergo surgical intervention, the number is roughly half that at about 33%. There are many reasons that a person may choose to undergo medical intervention, and there are just as many reasons that a person might choose not to. Surgical intervention can be costly and, for many, cost prohibitive.

With one-third of transgender individuals undergoing surgical intervention and two-thirds undergoing either surgical or hormonal intervention, it's important that you understand these procedures and what they entail. This is not a medical book, so the level of detail offered in these explanations will be minimal, with the goal being to support individuals who desire a rudimentary understanding of what these procedures entail. A more in-depth discussion is beyond the scope of this chapter and this book.

You will find in reading this section that many procedures and interventions are specific to gender. For example, a transgender man would receive phalloplasty, whereas a transgender woman would receive vaginoplasty. For this reason, interventions will be separated by gender in the following sections.

Transgender Men

A transgender man is an individual whose sex assigned at birth was female but whose gender identity is male. For this reason, when a transgender man undergoes medical transition, the procedures they undertake are meant to align their physical bodies with their masculine gender identity. Some of the mechanisms by which they do this are discussed below.

Hormone Therapy

Many transgender men will undergo masculinizing hormone therapy, which is achieved by administering testosterone. Testosterone can be administered in multiple ways, including injections, gels, patches, pellets under the skin, and orally through a pill. Hormone therapy is often referred to as a *second puberty*, because the outcome is the development of secondary sex characteristics, much as when an individual experiences their first puberty.

Some of the changes that you can expect when undergoing masculinizing hormone therapy are your skin becoming thicker and more oily, a change in body odor, increased perspiration, redistribution of subcutaneous fat, increased muscle definition, decrease in facial fat (which will allow for a more defined and angular facial appearance), thickening of the vocal cords (which results in a deepening of the voice), increased body hair (including hair on the chest, back, and arms), increased facial hair, and changes to the hair on your head (which can include frontal scalp hair thinning and male pattern baldness). There are also sexual implications of masculinizing hormone therapy, such as an increase in libido and enlarging of the clitoris, vaginal atrophy (when the lining of the vagina gets drier and thinner), and amenorrhea (no longer having a period).

While it is common to desire the effects of masculinizing hormone therapy to occur as soon as possible, the truth is these changes take time. For example, increased facial and body hair can take about three to six months to begin to show up and three to five years before you get the full effect of the testosterone. Sadly, that means it could take three to five years before you have that beard you were always hoping for, and even then the thickness and the pattern of your facial hair will be impacted by many things, including your genetics and overall health. Muscle mass and strength are similar in that it takes about

6 to 12 months to begin seeing the impact of testosterone in those areas and two to five years before you reach the maximum effect of the testosterone. The same is true for the redistribution of body fat, which takes about 3 to 6 months to begin to take effect and about two to five years to reach maximum effect. The deeper voice you always wanted takes about 3 to 12 months to begin to take effect and about one to two years before reaching full effect. Enlargement of the clitoris takes about 3 to 6 months to begin to take effect and about one to two years before reaching maximum effect, and these are just some examples.

It's important to note that some changes are only maintained through the continued use of testosterone, including the changes related to muscle mass, fat distribution, and menstruation. It is also important to note that the fact that you are on masculinizing hormone therapy does not necessarily mean that you will no longer be able to become pregnant. Some individuals are still able to achieve pregnancy despite the use of testosterone. For this reason, it's important that you utilize contraceptives in a manner consistent with your desire or lack of desire to become pregnant.

Hysterectomy

A hysterectomy is a surgery that removes all or part of the uterus as well as sometimes the ovaries and fallopian tubes. According to the National Transgender Discrimination Survey, roughly 20% of transgender men have had a hysterectomy, and just shy of 60% of transgender men desire to have a hysterectomy at some time in the future. There are many reasons that a transgender man might choose to have a hysterectomy. Some of these reasons include having their body come into better alignment with their gender identity, preventing menstruation, preventing gynecological visits and exams, and for preexisting and unrelated medical reasons.

Male Chest Reconstruction

Male chest reconstruction surgery, otherwise known as "female-to-male top surgery" or simply "top surgery," is the most common form of surgical intervention for transgender men. In most instances, when people refer to female-to-male top surgery, they are referring to bilateral mastectomy with chest reconstruction. There are multiple types of top surgery, including peri-areolar, keyhole, double incision with free nipple grafts, and double incision with inverted-T technique. Each of these procedures is performed under general anesthesia, takes roughly two to three hours to complete, and is performed on an outpatient basis.

Phalloplasty

Phalloplasty is the creation of a penis that is formed out of donor skin from the radial forearm or the anterior lateral thigh. Phalloplasty is a complex procedure requiring the donor skin to be rolled into a tube and grafted to the inguinal area. Phalloplasty often requires multiple surgeries. An erectile implant may be placed if so desired. It's important to note that the penis may or may not have sensation.

Additionally, you must have a hysterectomy (the removal of your uterus) and oophorectomy (the removal of your ovaries) prior to phalloplasty. Phalloplasty is an inpatient surgery. The surgery itself ranges from 6 to 8 hours in duration, and you will be expected to stay in the hospital for a minimum of four days but often up to seven days post-operation.

Metoidioplasty

As previously discussed, masculinizing hormone therapy through testosterone results in the enlargement of the clitoris. Metoidioplasty utilizes the enlarged clitoris to construct a penis, sometimes called a micropenis, as it is usually approximately 1 to 3 inches long with a girth roughly the size of someone's thumb. The surgery can take two to five hours, and individuals are likely to stay in the hospital for a day or two after surgery. The individual can also choose to include the surgical construction of a glans, which allows for a closer resemblance to a cisgender male's penis. They may also choose to undergo a urethroplasty, which is a lengthening of the urethra that will enable them to be able to urinate while standing up. Some choose to have a scrotoplasty completed simultaneously, which is the surgical creation of a scrotum from the labia majora. If desired, an individual can also receive testicular implants.

Vaginectomy

A vaginectomy is a form of bottom surgery that removes the vaginal lining and closes the vagina. A vaginectomy eliminates the need for future gynecological examinations and removes the experience of vaginal secretions. Both can be experienced as positive side effects of the procedure for transgender men. A vaginectomy is an inpatient procedure performed under general anesthesia and requires a hospital stay of approximately one week.

Transgender Women

A transgender woman is an individual whose sex assigned at birth is male but whose gender identity is female. When a transgender woman undergoes medical transition, the procedures that they undertake are meant to align their physical bodies with their gender identity. Some of the mechanisms by which they do this are discussed below.

Feminizing Hormone Therapy

Many transgender women will undergo feminizing hormone therapy. Three widely utilized forms of feminizing hormone therapy are estrogen, testosterone blockers, and progesterone. Estrogen is the primary female hormone and is responsible for many of the changes you see in a person medically transitioning from male to female. Estrogen can be administered in multiple ways, including by pill, injection, gel, spray, or patch. Testosterone blockers are also known as anti-androgens. The purpose of a testosterone blocker is to stop the production and action of testosterone in the body. Progesterone is a hormone found in cisgender women that can be prescribed to transgender women; it is thought to improve mood and enhance breast development and body fat redistribution, although there is not much conclusive clinical evidence to support this. Progesterone can also be used as a partial testosterone blocker. Individuals typically are not prescribed progesterone until their hormone levels have stabilized on estrogen.

Hormone therapy is often referred to as second puberty because of the development of secondary sex characteristics consistent with the hormones that are being prescribed. For example, for transgender women, some of the changes that you can expect are decreased perspiration, thinner skin, smaller pores, and breast development. While breast development is a common side effect of feminizing hormone therapy, it's important to note that you are not likely to develop large breasts. Most transgender women will not develop breasts larger than an A cup or possibly a very small B cup. If a person is not pleased with the size of their breasts after having stabilized on feminizing hormones, breast augmentation is an option that can be considered after having been on hormones for at least one year.

Additionally, transgender women will experience a decrease in their muscle mass as well as a decrease in their strength. They will begin to collect fat in areas consistent with cisgender women, such as the hips and thighs, and the appearance of the face will become less angular as fat underneath the skin increases and shifts. Hair on the face and chest will begin to thin, although it will not likely go away entirely. Also, unlike the impact of testosterone on the voice of transgender men, feminizing hormone therapy does not affect the tone and tenor of the transgender woman's voice.

Additionally, there are sexual side effects of feminizing hormone therapy, which include a decrease in the number of erections, a decrease in the firmness of erections (which can cause it to be challenging to perform penetration), a decrease in the amount of time an erection lasts once achieved, testicle shrinkage (in which testicles will often shrink to less than half of their original size), and notably the possibility of lowering sperm count, which is something that should be taken into consideration if you think that you might want to parent a child from your sperm in the future. The fact that you are on feminizing hormone therapy does not mean that you are unable to get someone pregnant. So you should utilize contraceptives in a manner consistent with your desire or lack of desire to parent a child from your sperm.

Orchiectomy

Transgender women may decide to have an orchiectomy, the surgical removal of one or both testicles. Once an individual has completed an orchiectomy, the body no longer produces testosterone, removing the need for testosterone blockers and possibly reducing the amount of estrogen necessary to achieve maximum benefit. After an orchiectomy, the body also no longer creates sperm, resulting in sterility. Orchiectomies are performed under general anesthesia on an outpatient basis and take approximately 30–60 minutes to complete.

Tracheal Shave

A tracheal shave is a surgical procedure in which the notch on the thyroid cartilage is removed, lessening the appearance of the Adam's apple. The procedure is completed under general anesthesia on an outpatient basis, typically taking 30–60 minutes to complete.

Facial Feminization Surgery

Transgender women may choose to complete facial feminization surgery. Several different procedures fall into this category, and a person may choose to complete all, some, or none of these procedures. Some procedures include forehead and hairline contouring, brow lift and eyelid lift, cheek augmentation, rhinoplasty (colloquially referred to as a nose job), lip lift and augmentation, jaw angle reduction, and chin width reduction. There are also nonsurgical procedures such as liposuction, fat grafting, injectables, and fillers.

Voice Feminization Surgery

Transgender women may opt to complete voice feminization surgery to make the voice sound more typical of a woman. Unlike testosterone's deepening of the voice for transgender men, estrogen does not make the voice higher. For this reason, some people undergo voice training to assist them with achieving the desired tone of voice. In some instances, voice training is sufficient to reach your desired goal. Other times, individuals find that the techniques learned during voice training fall short of reaching their desired goal, and they may choose to undergo voice feminization surgery. There are multiple types of voice feminization surgery, including cricothyroid approximation (which tenses and lengthens the vocal folds), anterior commissure advancement or Wendler glottoplasty (which shortens the vibrating length of the vocal folds), laser-assisted voice adjustment (which makes the vocal folds smaller and tenser), and laser reduction glottoplasty (which causes the vocal folds to become more tense).

Vaginoplasty

The most common form of vaginoplasty is penile inversion vaginoplasty. This procedure creates a vaginal canal between the rectum and the urethra, in which the vaginal lining is created from penile skin. An orchiectomy (the removal of the testicles) is performed, and the skin of the scrotum is used to create the labia majora. The clitoris is constructed using a portion of the glans penis. Vaginoplasty is performed on an inpatient basis under general anesthesia. Most individuals will stay in the hospital for a minimum of three days after the procedure. Vaginoplasty requires postoperative care to include a dilation schedule that decreases frequency over time.

Breast Augmentation

As stated previously, transgender women can experience breast growth due to feminizing hormone therapy. However, it is not likely that they will grow large breasts. Instead, they are likely to develop breasts that are an A cup or perhaps a small B cup. If a person desires larger breasts, they may opt for breast augmentation, which is the placement of breast implants underneath the breast tissue and muscle. Most surgeons require that a transgender woman undergo estrogen therapy for a minimum of 12 months before the surgery. A full recovery from breast augmentation surgery usually takes four to six weeks.

Interventions Used by Both Transgender Men and Women

Some procedures are employed by both transgender men and women, although the target of the intervention and the desired outcome may differ. Both hair removal and voice and speech therapy are often sought by both transgender men and women, albeit for different reasons, and these differences are discussed below.

Hair Removal

People often think of transgender women when they think of hair removal. For example, transgender women often utilize laser hair removal or electrolysis to remove unwanted hair from the face, neck, chest, and back. They may also seek hair removal in the genital area in preparation for vaginoplasty. Transgender men also seek hair removal in preparation for phalloplasty. The donor skin (typically taken from the forearm or thigh) must be hairless to prevent hair growth in the urethra.

Voice and Speech Therapy

People often think of transgender women when they think of the use of voice and speech therapy for transgender individuals. This is in part because feminizing hormone therapy does not change the pitch of the voice. While it is true that transgender women may undergo voice and speech therapy in an effort to feminize their voice, it is also the case that transgender men often pursue voice and speech therapy as well because even though masculinizing hormone therapy does cause the voice to deepen, sometimes the changes do not reach the desired effect and the individual has to learn techniques to further shift the tone and tenor of their voice.

Legal Transition

Legal transition is a form of transition that many people fail to fully consider. The process of legal transition can be both costly and time-consuming. Imagine having to change your information on every document upon which you have ever been identified. People often consider that individuals have to change current documentation but overlook the necessity of altering previous documentation to be consistent with the now-recognized identity. I will attempt to differentiate between these two documentation classes and hope you will be able to see why both are valuable.

Current Documentation

Current documentation is the documentation that you generally need to perform activities and function in daily life:

- Driver's license or state ID card
- Car registration and insurance
- Credit and debit cards
- Credit reports
- Bank accounts
- Mortgage documents or leases
- Social Security records
- Birth certificate
- Passport
- Work visa
- Green card

- Government benefits cards
- Wills and care directives
- Durable powers of attorney
- Professional licenses
- Resumes and online professional profiles
- Health and dental insurance

Depending on a person's life and circumstances, other forms of documentation might also exist.

Previous Documentation

Previous documentation is the documentation that has been established in the past but that you don't generally need to perform regular activities in daily life:

- School transcripts and diplomas
- Marriage license
- Children's birth certificates
- Military service records
- Veterans' Administration records
- Employment records
- Medical records
- Court documents, such as custody agreements or lawsuit paperwork

At first glance, you may not understand the importance of changing historical documentation to be consistent with your current identity. Failing to do so can make situations more difficult and open you up to the unintended consequence of outing yourself when that is not your desire.

For example, let's say you have applied for a job and have successfully interviewed. The company decides that they want to move forward with your candidacy, but first they must check with your previous employer to ensure you are eligible for rehire. Suppose you have not changed your name in your previous employer's system. In that case, when your potential employer calls and asks about your eligibility for rehire, they will likely be told that they have never had an employee by that name (your current name) because you are in the system using your former name.

Another example concerns attempts to obtain your medical records when your current name does not match the name in the system. You can see how these situations can very easily become troublesome. Likewise, there can be issues when trying to enroll your child in school if the name on your driver's license does not match your parental name on their birth certificate. One more example – one that hits close to home for me – is changing your name on your diplomas. I have three degrees, but you will never see them displayed on my wall because they bear my deadname. I have tried to have this corrected, but unless I legally change my name, my university is unable to do so. So instead of celebrating what is definitely an accomplishment worth celebrating, I hide my diplomas.

Now that we understand transition on a basic level, we can discuss how to make the transition process as comfortable as possible in the workplace. One way that we can do that is by not requiring our transgender employees to be the resident subject matter experts and to answer our questions on the topic. Asking them to do so is not only wildly inappropriate, but it can very well cause emotional harm on the part of the transgender individual. Should you seek answers to your questions? Sure. Should you seek them from your transgender colleague? No. That is where this book comes in.

Chapter 4

Questions About Medical Transition

We, as a people, appear to have a collective fascination with medical experiences – so much so that there are television shows, radio shows, podcasts, and websites dedicated exclusively to that very topic. We want to understand the medical experiences that might directly apply to ourselves or our loved ones, but we also have a broader curiosity about the human condition in general. Many individuals have questions about the medical transition of individuals in the transgender community, and this chapter will seek to answer some of those questions.

What Percentage of Transgender People Transition Medically?

According to the United States Transgender Survey, 78% of transgender individuals desire hormone therapy related to gender transition. Having said that, only 49% of transgender individuals have ever actually received hormone therapy. For individuals who have undergone some form of transition-related surgery, the number is even smaller: 25%. Additionally, it is important to note that transgender men are more likely than transgender women to have transition-related surgery. Not surprisingly, individuals who live in poverty, have a low income, or are uninsured are less likely to have transition-related surgery. Mastectomy is the most common surgical intervention, with the least common surgical intervention being phalloplasty.

Why Do Some Transgender People Not Do Every Possible Medical Transition?

There are many reasons that a person may choose some medical transitions and not others. For starters, some individuals might not feel like they need all of the available options in order to embody their full selves. For example, some will have top surgery but will opt out of having bottom surgery. In some cases, it's simply because they don't feel like they need bottom surgery in order to walk in the fullness of who they are. There are also times when individuals opt to undergo hormone replacement therapy but choose not to have any surgical interventions because the effects of the hormones are enough for them to feel as though they have found a place of alignment and synergy.

We must also take into consideration financial means. Surgical intervention can be very expensive, and an individual might be able to afford hormone replacement therapy but not be able to afford corresponding surgical intervention. While many insurance policies will cover gender-affirming surgery, many others don't, or their coverage is limited. It is also essential to remember that transgender individuals are less likely than their cisgender counterparts to be insured as a direct result of the likelihood of them being underemployed or unemployed.

What's more, there is often a lot of red tape to get through before an insurance company will cover gender-affirming services. It's also the case that hormone replacement therapy is often thought of as the first step in medical transition, and so a person who is interested in surgical intervention might not be able to access it without first undergoing hormone replacement therapy. This prerequisite can act as a deterrent for individuals who would like to undergo surgical intervention but do not desire hormone replacement therapy. This is frequently the case with individuals who identify as nonbinary. For example, a nonbinary person who was assigned female at birth may want to undergo top surgery so that they can have a more androgynous physique but might not desire to undergo hormone replacement therapy, which would cause them to develop the secondary sex characteristics of a man, which is actually counter to their desire to appear androgynous.

It is also the case that surgical interventions carry with them a heightened level of risk, such as the risk of complications during the healing process and the risk of negative impact on the ability to experience pleasure during sexual exchanges. One example of this is phalloplasty, which we discussed in Chapter 3. Often, individuals who undergo phalloplasty find that they don't have the same level of sensitivity on their penis as they did previously on their clitoris. This decreased sensitivity can lead to less sexual pleasure during sexual experiences.

Also, a person may simply feel as though they have reached their desired outcome and might not feel the need to go any further in terms of medical transition. For example, a transgender man might be satisfied with the enlargement of the clitoris that takes place by virtue of hormone replacement therapy and not feel as though they need to move on to metoidioplasty or phalloplasty. Another example of this would be a transgender woman who feels as though they have reached their desired outcome after undergoing breast augmentation and does not feel they need to have bottom surgery.

If the desire is to pass as a member of the gender that you identify with, you might not feel as though every available option is necessary to achieve that goal. For example, a transgender man might undergo hormone replacement therapy and experience the broadening of the shoulders, the deepening of the voice, and the development of facial hair, and might find that that, coupled with binding their chest, is sufficient for them to pass as a cisgender man. If the goal is passing and passing alone, they might not feel the need to move forward and have top surgery, and even if they did feel the need to move forward and have top surgery, they might find it unnecessary to have bottom surgery because where large breasts are often easily visible even if you are binding your chest, your lower genitalia is not readily noticeable. Similarly, a transgender woman may feel comfortable simply wearing a padded bra and tucking. If that alone is sufficient for them to pass as a cisgender woman, they might choose not to undergo surgical intervention at all.

It is also the case that some may struggle with the fact that insurance companies often necessitate that you characterize your transgender identity as an illness before they pay for medical intervention. Stated differently, most insurance companies require that you have a medical diagnosis of gender dysphoria before they pay for you to receive gender-affirming services. The use of the medical model necessitates that you self-identify as ill so that you may receive services. This can be a very tough pill to swallow for individuals who don't feel as though they are sick. I personally struggled with this requirement. In order for me to begin hormone replacement therapy I had to receive a diagnosis of gender dysphoria. The first time I saw my diagnosis written on a piece of paper,

I struggled a great deal. The endocrinologist was saying that I was sick, that something was wrong with me, and it needed to be fixed. I experienced a great deal of distress when I came to that realization because, while I felt as though I was in a body that was inconsistent with who I knew myself to be, I never viewed myself as ill, and not just ill but chronically ill, such that I needed long-lasting remediation. Having them indicate that I needed to be fixed was probably just as damaging as any transphobic rhetoric I had heard up to that point. As far as I was concerned, I didn't experience gender dysphoria in the classical sense; instead, I had this deep-rooted awareness that I was not in the right body. I didn't hate my body. It just wasn't the right one. So in many ways, I'm a very good example of someone who might not opt to employ every possible intervention. Because for me, it's less about ridding myself of things that I dislike and more about having the opportunity to embrace pieces of myself that I've not yet been able to access.

Is It Expensive to Transition Medically?

Medical transition can be very expensive; in fact, the cost of transitioning medically can be so great that for some, the process is cost prohibitive. It's important to understand that in the context of transitioning medically, you're not just talking about the completion of the procedures. You must also bear in mind all of the money spent in the period before transition, ensuring that you meet the requirements, as well as the money spent post-medical intervention to ensure that you experience and maintain the desired results.

To answer this question adequately, we need to provide a bit of a road map. We must have a focal point so that we can discuss this topic in appropriate segments, so we will look at expenses as occurring in two separate phases. The first phase consists of any medical interventions that are needed as a prerequisite to gender-affirming surgery. The second phase is the gender-affirming surgery itself. Let's jump on in and answer the question.

Preoperative Expenses

Often, insurance companies, as well as providers, will require that an individual meet specific requirements prior to either agreeing to pay for surgery (in the case of the insurance company) or agreeing to perform the surgery (in the case of the provider). One fairly standard prerequisite for surgery is a formal diagnosis of gender dysphoria. Obtaining that diagnosis frequently has inherent costs associated with it. If you receive this diagnosis from a mental health therapist, they often require several visits with you prior to providing a definitive diagnosis. Therapy costs can range from relatively small copays of $25 up to out-of-pocket costs of $150 to $200 per session. If you met with a psychologist or psychiatrist, you might receive that diagnosis based on one meeting, but one appointment with a psychologist or a psychiatrist can easily cost you several hundred dollars.

Many insurance plans, as well as surgeons, require that an individual be undergoing hormone replacement therapy for a minimum of one year before either paying for or performing the surgery. Prior to being prescribed hormones, your physician is likely going to order a comprehensive blood panel to get a sense of your current levels and to assess for any other areas of concern. If you don't have insurance, this blood panel can easily cost several hundred dollars, possibly even $1,000 or more.

Additionally, the cost of hormones can add up very quickly. Using myself as an example, when I began the process of medical transition, I started hormone therapy. I was prescribed testosterone. The preferred method of application for me was through a testosterone gel, essentially a topical treatment. Just to give you an idea of how quickly expenses can add up, a 90-day supply of my testosterone gel costs $1,038.99 out of pocket. Fortunately I had insurance, although getting my insurance to pay for it was a bit difficult in that it required a prior authorization because it was a topical application as opposed to an injection, which would have been less expensive but for me was contraindicated.

My situation is not unique; many people find hormone replacement therapy to be expensive, and this isn't just for transgender men, but this is also the case for transgender women. When it comes to hormone replacement therapy, the delivery method directly impacts the cost. For example, oral estrogen can easily be obtained for less than $100 a month; however, injectable estrogen is likely to run $150 to $200 a month. Similarly, testosterone injections typically cost less than $100 a month, whereas patches can easily run more than $300 a month and gels even more than that. Again in my case, testosterone gel was over $1,000 for a 90-day supply.

The Cost of Surgical Intervention

The costs increase substantially when it comes to surgical intervention. Even with insurance, a person can easily spend thousands of dollars in copays, coinsurance, and/or deductibles. Gender-affirming surgery is so expensive that many uninsured people cannot afford it. (See the previous chapter for explanations of the different types of surgeries.)

Let's discuss a few procedures and their cost related to transgender men. Top surgery is a fairly common procedure, but that does not mean it's inexpensive. In fact, top surgery costs roughly between $8,000 and $12,000. But that's nowhere near as expensive as metoidioplasty, which can easily run between $50,000 and $60,000, or phalloplasty, which can easily run between $50,000 and $300,000. Often, when people are thinking about surgical intervention for transgender individuals, they're thinking about genitalia, but another procedure that transgender men opt to undergo at times is a hysterectomy, which can easily cost between $10,000 and $12,000.

But these expenses aren't just limited to transgender men. Transgender women also pay a great deal for gender-affirming surgery. The cost of breast augmentation can be anywhere from $5,000 to $10,000. If an individual decides to get facial feminization surgery, that can cost up to $50,000, with the cost being highly dependent on the preexisting bone structure of the individual. If a transgender woman decides to have a vaginoplasty, that can range between $35,000 and $55,000, and labioplasties often cost an additional $4,000 to $6,000. An orchiectomy also ranges from around $4,000 to $6,000.

If medical transition sounds expensive, that's because it is. According to the Philadelphia Center for transgender surgery, medically transitioning from male to female costs roughly $140,450, and transitioning from female to male costs roughly $124,400. To put this in perspective, you can purchase a home in many states for less than the cost of medical transition.

And the expenses don't suddenly stop once a person undergoes transition-related surgery. The truth is there will likely be follow-up appointments and there is often a desire to continue hormone replacement therapy. The cost of post-surgical care is a little tough to anticipate, however, as the desire or need can vary widely.

Can You Transition Back If You Change Your Mind?

Detransitioning is when a person returns to living as the gender they were thought to be at birth after having previously transitioned to living as the gender that was consistent with their gender identity. According to the U.S. Trans Survey, 8% of transgender individuals who have transitioned socially or otherwise have detransitioned, and of those, most have only done so temporarily. In fact, 62% of the individuals who reported that they detransitioned had retransitioned by the time of the survey and were currently living in a manner consistent with their gender identity.

Transgender women were more likely than transgender men to report having detransitioned at a rate of 11% and 4%, respectively. What's more, when asked why they chose to detransition, the reasons were numerous and were not what some may have expected. For example, only 5% of individuals who detransitioned said they did so because they realized that they should not have transitioned in the first place. Conversely, the most common reason for detransition, at 36%, was pressure from a parent, 26% was due to pressure from another family member, and 18% because of pressure from their spouse or partner. Additionally, 31% reported having detransitioned as a result of harassment or discrimination, and 29% reported having detransitioned as a result of having trouble getting a job. When all of that is taken into consideration, you find that very few transgender individuals detransition, and those who do largely do so as a result of pressure, harassment, or discrimination.

How Often Do People Regret Transition-Related Surgeries?

According to Bustos and colleagues, who conducted a meta-analysis published in *Plastic and Reconstructive Surgery – Global Open* in 2021 that reviewed 27 studies assessing a total of 7,928 transgender individuals from 14 countries who underwent transition-related surgery, the prevalence of surgery-related regret is very, very low. In fact, the meta-analysis found that for those having undergone transmasculine surgeries, the rate of regret was less than 1%, and for those having undergone transfeminine surgeries, the rate of regret was 1%. Regarding specific procedures, the study found that 2% of individuals experienced regret after a vaginoplasty, whereas less than 1% of individuals experienced regret after a mastectomy.

What Are the Most Common Complications from Transgender Surgery?

According to a study published in 2018 by Lane and colleagues, which can be found in *Plastic and Reconstructive Surgery – Global Open,* there was a complication rate of 5.8% in transgender patients who underwent surgical procedures. Not all procedures carry the same rate of complication: the highest rate of complication occurring with phalloplasty and the lowest rate in orchiectomy. The most common complication was wound infection.

Does Health Insurance Cover Medical Transition?

Before we discuss the extent to which health insurance covers medical transition, we should first discuss what percentage of the transgender community has health insurance. According to the U.S. Trans Survey, 86% of transgender individuals report being covered by a health insurance plan, whereas 14% report being uninsured. These numbers are lower than what is found in the general population, in which 89% of adults in the United States report being covered by health insurance, with only 11% reporting being uninsured.

There were also differences found in terms of insurance coverage based on region and ethnicity. More specifically, individuals in the South were more likely to be uninsured than other members of the study, and Black individuals were more likely to be uninsured than any other race represented in the study. Even more concerning is the fact that individuals who were not U.S. citizens were less likely to be insured, with 24% of documented non-U.S. citizens reporting being uninsured and a striking 58% of undocumented residents reporting being uninsured.

Regardless, having health insurance does not necessarily mean that you have access to gender-affirming care. The survey found that 55% of transgender individuals who seek transition-related surgery are denied coverage by their health insurance plan, and 25% of those who seek hormone replacement therapy are denied by their health insurance plan. Additionally, transgender men were more likely to be denied insurance coverage for transition-related surgery as well as for hormones than transgender women.

What Are Some Ways to Transition Medically That Do Not Involve Surgery?

The most popular form of medical transition that does not involve surgery is hormone replacement therapy. As explained previously, individuals can choose to medically transition by introducing masculinizing or feminizing hormones. Hormone therapy can result in changes that are physical, emotional, sexual, and reproductive. For some individuals, these changes may be sufficient to effectively combat gender dysphoria, and they might not desire to undergo surgical intervention.

Since this chapter is focused on medical transition, I will briefly discuss some of the physical effects of hormone replacement therapy. For individuals undergoing feminizing hormone therapy, some of these effects are the development of breast tissue, decreased perspiration, decrease in muscle tone, thinning of both facial hair and chest hair, testicle shrinkage, experiencing fewer erections, and collection of fat in the hip and thigh area. For individuals undergoing masculinizing hormone therapy, common physical effects are increased perspiration, acne, a deepening of the voice, increased muscle definition, redistribution of fat away from hips and thighs, changes in libido, and changes in the menstrual cycle to include shorter periods that for many will eventually stop altogether.

This is not an exhaustive list (a more comprehensive list is found elsewhere in the book), but the subject is mentioned here to show that even without surgical intervention, an individual can experience a lot of physical changes even if their medical transition is limited to hormone replacement therapy.

How Can Human Resources Support Someone in the Process of Medical Transition?

Human resource professionals play a vital role in the creation and maintenance of a work culture that is both safe and affirming for transgender individuals. One way that human resources can support those who are medically transitioning is to be proactive in cultivating a trans-affirming environment. Do not wait until an employee comes to you and informs you that they are medically transitioning to begin to assess your policies and procedures. Do you have clear guidelines in place for medical transition? Have you outlined the roles and responsibilities of employees at every level of the organization? What about your health-care benefits? Be proactive and assess your healthcare benefits; do they cover transition-related services? If so, are there unnecessary prerequisites that must be met in order for a person to access coverage? For example, a transgender man is made to receive hormone therapy for one year prior to the authorization of a mastectomy. How about your leave policies? Can you ensure that a transgender employee will not lose their job for taking the necessary time to heal post-surgical intervention?

This chapter is not meant to be an exhaustive list of questions, but I hope that these answers, coupled with the information provided earlier in the book, serve as a good start on your quest to better understand medical transition.

Medical transition clearly impacts a person both at home and in the workplace. Another form of transition that impacts most areas of a person's life is legal transition, which is the form of transition we will discuss next.

Chapter 5

Questions About Legal Transition

Legal transition can be both time and resource intensive.

Many individuals underestimate the process of legal transition, thinking it is limited to the changing of a person's name and perhaps their gender marker. But there is so much more that goes into a comprehensive legal transition, and this chapter will highlight this as well as explore some of the ways in which the process is beyond reach for some. Now let's jump into the questions.

What Percentage of Transgender Individuals Transition Legally?

According to the 2015 U.S. Transgender Survey, many members of the transgender community desire to change their name or gender markers on their identifying documents but are unable to do so. In fact, the survey found that only 11% of respondents had their chosen name and gender on all of their documentation, whereas 68% did not have their chosen name and gender on any of their documentation. They also found that changing your name or gender markers on your driver's license was less difficult than changing it on your birth certificate; consequently, whereas 29% of those who desired to change their gender on their driver's license or state ID were able to do so, only 9% were able to do so on their birth certificate. Why do these numbers matter? It is important to realize that if a person transitions socially or medically but does not transition legally they may find themselves in a situation where others find out that they are transgender simply by seeing their driver license or passport. This can make for a potentially dangerous situation, particularly if the person who is becoming aware that you are transgender harbors hostile feelings toward the transgender community.

If we aren't careful we can view the inability to change your identifying documents as nothing more than an inconvenience; I mean, how often do you have to show your ID? Well, the reality is there are many aspects of our life that require us to provide identification, such as if you want to buy alcohol or cigarettes, if you want to get a hotel room or rent a car, or perhaps most germane to this book, when you're onboarding at a new job.

Is It Expensive to Transition Legally?

To answer this question, we must first acknowledge that what one person experiences as expensive might not be the same for another person. You'll recall that I mentioned earlier that transgender individuals are more likely to be unemployed or underemployed than their cisgender counterparts. This lack of access to financial resources could make transitioning legally more difficult for a member of the transgender community than a member of the general population. Having said that, and to provide some context, according to the U.S. Trans Survey, 34% percent of those who had obtained a legal name change indicated that they had spent over $250 and 11% reported having spent over $500. It's also important to bear in mind that while transitioning, one item might not be particularly expensive; if an individual is to go through a comprehensive legal transition and is expected to pay a wide variety of fees, the financial burden may be cumulative.

What Are Some of the Reasons That People Choose Not to Transition Legally?

There are many reasons that a person may choose not to transition legally. One reason we have just discussed is lack of financial resources. A person may not have the means to pay all the fees associated with legal transition. There are also other reasons that a person might not choose to transition legally. Sometimes a person's legal name has great significance to them or their family, which might cause them to be reluctant to change their name.

I will use myself as an example of this. When I transitioned socially, I began asking people to refer to me as A.C., which is not my given name but my chosen name. When I initially began requesting that people refer to me as A.C. I received some pushback from someone I deeply cherished. A close relative of mine took issue with the fact that I no longer wanted to use my given name. I can't speak for them, but their response gave me the impression that they viewed it as a personal slight. And that, of course, was not at all my aim. I simply wanted to distance myself from my given name because that name is highly gendered, and I have found that I am misgendered more often when people see my given name. I tried my best to explain this and even pointed out that A.C. were, in fact, my initials, and so while I might be distancing myself from my given name, I had not given up on it entirely. That said, I've been running into issues in certain areas of my life because I have not legally changed my name, and thus I have to interface with my given name in some instances. Those experiences have caused me to experience significant dysphoria, so for that reason, even though I'm reluctant to change my name, I might very well go about the process of doing so in order to lessen the frequency with which I come into contact with my deadname and the frequency with which I am misgendered.

Another reason that a person might choose not to transition legally could be concerns for their safety. For example, if you change the gender markers on your identification but you have the secondary sex characteristics of the sex that you were assigned at birth, you might find yourself inadvertently being outed anytime someone comes into contact with your identification.

A person might also simply not desire to transition legally because they don't see it as something necessary or important to them. For many years I felt this way. It was enough for me to transition socially; it didn't really bother me that my gender markers were consistent with my sex assigned at birth on my identification or that my legal name was on my birth certificate. None of that really bothered me because the people that I came into contact with on a daily basis honored my pronouns and my chosen name, so I didn't have to interface very often with my given name or the gender consistent with my sex assigned at birth. However, as time progressed, something began to change for me. I began to experience greater and more significant dysphoria associated with being called my given name or seeing a gender marker on my identification that was consistent with my sex assigned at birth as opposed to my gender identity. I say this because had you known me some years ago, you would have known someone who had very little, if any, interest in legally transitioning, but now I am strongly considering it.

Another reason that a person might choose not to legally transition could be that their given name has significance to them in other ways. For example, let's say that you are a person with a child, and your child has been named after you, or perhaps even you were named after someone, that might very well cause you to be reluctant to change your name because of the association with a person you love.

Additionally, some people have spent a long time establishing their careers, and their name is linked to their brand identity. It's important to maintain their brand identity exactly as it is for a variety of reasons: so former business associates can again find them, so word-of-mouth clients can find them, so their existing clients feel reassured by ongoing consistency and stability in dealing with them, so changing long-standing contractual relationships doesn't cause partner organizations headaches, and so on. These are often the same reasons people retain their surnames when they get married or divorced.

What Advice Would You Give Someone Who Wants to Transition Legally but Doesn't Know Where to Begin?

This might not be the advice that you would get from someone else, but my personal opinion is that if you choose to transition legally and you have the means to do so, prioritize the items that are most distressing for you. For example, if hearing or seeing your deadname is highly distressing, focus on legally changing your name as a place to start so that you can lessen your experience of distress and dysphoria. If being referred to as the gender that is associated with the sex you were assigned at birth really bothers you, then consider changing your gender marker on your identification first. The decision ultimately lies with the person who is choosing to transition legally, but given the opportunity to choose a starting place, I would begin by addressing the area that is causing me the most harm.

How Can Human Resources Support People Through Legal Transition?

The first thing that human resources can do is not require a legal transition to honor a person's chosen name and pronouns. Legal transition is not readily accessible for some people, and when you require legal transition before you will honor a person's chosen name and pronouns, you place them in a position where if they are unable to transition legally, they are unable to experience a basic level of decency and respect at their place of employment. So first things first: do not require that a person legally transition before you begin using their chosen name and pronouns on all of your materials, both outward-facing and inward-facing. Do not require that a person transition legally before you respect and honor them for who they are.

Getting a person's name right is a sign of basic respect, as is getting their pronouns right. When you get a person's name and pronouns correct, what you are conveying to them is *I see you, I affirm you, and I value you.*

Failure to do that sends a very different message, and I would argue that the meta-communication there is that I do not see you as you know yourself to be, or I am unwilling to take the necessary steps to make sure that you are not experiencing unnecessary distress. Might it seem difficult at times to tailor your processes to the needs of a transgender employee? Sure. But we do things all the time that initially seem difficult, and we often discover that they're easier than we expected, and we become stronger for learning how to do them. Does it take some awareness to figure out how to get automated reports and outputs to reflect a person's chosen name instead of their given name? Sure. But we can do it. You must care enough to get it done. And with all of the resources that organizations have available to them today, you will be hard-pressed to convince someone that you have tried in earnest if you are unable to honor something as simple as a chosen name and pronouns.

Another consideration is that transitioning legally can be expensive, so if your organization can assist in paying fees for individuals who are legally transitioning, that would be a huge value add. Again, it's not often that one item is by itself cost prohibitive, but the accumulation of several items can be cost-prohibitive. So if there are funds to assist individuals to pay the application fees and the registration fees, and the administration fees associated with changing their documentation, that would be wonderful.

Next, there must be unambiguous policies and procedures around the use of chosen names and gender pronouns. It's important that your organization have a zero-tolerance policy for intentional misgendering or deadnaming. Not only must this be expressed in your policies, but it's also important that your policies actually be utilized as the basis for progressive discipline in the instance that a person is intentionally deadnaming or misgendering a person who is transgender or nonbinary. This should be the case whether or not a person has legally transitioned. That is to say, whether or not your driver's license has your chosen name on it, individuals who work with you should be expected to refer to you utilizing your chosen name; similarly, whether or not your driver's license has the gender marker consistent with your gender identity, individuals should be expected to refer to you utilizing the pronouns that are consistent with your gender identity. Failure to do so should be viewed as a contextual/citizenship performance issue. Some organizations view it as bullying; others view it as harassment. Whatever the framing, it should be considered a progressive discipline issue if a person intentionally misgenders or deadnames someone.

Also, suppose a person chooses to legally transition prior to having socially transitioned. In that case, they may need the assistance of human resources when it comes to letting other employees, superiors, or subordinates know that they have changed their name or gender markers. Human resources might be called on to assist with messaging as well as the provision of resources for individuals who might have additional questions. An employee should not be left to fend for themselves when it comes to answering questions. Human resources should serve as a buffer by either answering questions or providing a subject matter expert to do so.

Whether or not a person transitions legally should not be utilized as a meterstick for the validity of their identity. It is important that you understand that a person who does not transition legally is just as valid as someone who does. I recently found myself in a conversation with an HR executive about the negative impact that deadnaming and misgendering has on a transgender person. I was explaining that a company should not require legal transition to honor a person's chosen name and pronouns. The executive looked me square in my face and said, "Best practice is for a person to legally change their name." Sadly, this perspective, albeit faulty, is not surprising. He – the very person charged with creating a safe and affirming space for employees – was completely out of touch with the fact that legal transition is often difficult to attain, and when we require that we cause unnecessary harm.

This chapter is not an exhaustive list but is meant to serve as a sneak peek into the time- and resource-intensive process of legal transition. Not all individuals have the means to transition medically or legally, in part because of the time and money needed to do both. However, social transition is often more easily attainable, and that is the form of transition we will speak about next.

Chapter 6

Questions About Social Transition

While people often think of medical transition when they hear that a transgender person is "transitioning," for most transgender individuals, social transition takes place long before the medical transition (if medical transition ever takes place at all). This chapter is dedicated to answering some common questions about social transition.

What Percentage of Transgender People Transition Socially?

To answer this we must first define transition. To this end, I will focus on the 2015 U.S. Transgender Survey, the largest survey of transgender individuals in the United States to date. This study defined transition as living full-time in a gender that is different from the gender associated with the sex you were assigned at birth. What's interesting is that the survey found that most transgender people either already lived full-time as the gender consistent with their gender identity (62%) or they desired to someday (22%); 13% reported that they were unsure if they wanted to transition and 3% reported that they did not desire to do so. So data indicates that 84% of transgender folks have either already transitioned socially or desire to do so at some juncture.

What's the Difference Between a "Tomboy" and a Transgender Person Transitioning Socially?

An individual who is transgender has a gender identity that is inconsistent with the sex that they were assigned at birth. This differs from someone who may colloquially be referred to as a tomboy; typically, when someone is referring to a tomboy, they're simply saying that this individual behaves or dresses in ways inconsistent with gender stereotypes. You'll note that definition has nothing to do with gender identity and everything to do with adherence to strict societal gender norms. Whereas a tomboy might enjoy engaging in activities that are stereotypically deemed masculine, a transgender male would identify as a male, as opposed to simply enjoying traditionally masculine activities.

What's the Difference Between an Effeminate Man and a Transgender Person Transitioning Socially?

As stated above, being transgender is a matter of gender identity. It's a matter of who you know yourself to be, not simply gender expression or mannerisms. A man who presents with stereotypically feminine mannerisms would not be considered transgender unless they actually identified as a woman or something other than a man. Gender identity and gender expression are not synonymous. This question highlights a tendency to view things as gendered that are, perhaps, best not viewed in those terms. For example, what value is there in identifying mannerisms as masculine or feminine? It is this characterization of mannerisms that would cause someone to even refer to a man as effeminate, but that's a different discussion and beyond the scope of this book. In the meantime, suffice it to say that being transgender is a matter of gender identity; it is a matter of self-identification. Simply being viewed as too feminine or masculine is insufficient to deem someone transgender.

Is Transitioning Socially Easier Than Transitioning Legally or Medically?

I would not refer to any form of gender-related transition as easy. But I think what people are getting at when they ask this question is an attempt to better understand the barriers to transition that individuals experience when seeking to transition socially, legally, or medically. When framed in this way, my response to this question is that social transition is often more accessible to individuals than legal or medical transition. Medical transition, as we discussed, can be very expensive, and as a result, some people may find that they cannot afford this. Legal transition can be a very long and complicated process, which can also be expensive. Social transition can be expensive in some ways – for example, the purchasing of a new wardrobe if you so desire – but it can also be inexpensive (financially anyway) in other ways, such as utilizing a chosen name or asking individuals to respect your pronouns. And even though there are some costs associated with social transition, those costs are often much less than the cost associated with medical transition. So is any form of transition easy? No. But social transition is often less cost prohibitive than its legal and medical counterparts.

What If You Transition Socially, but You Change Your Mind?

A person can detransition after having transitioned socially just as they can detransition after having transitioned legally or medically. When it comes to detransitioning, social detransition is likely the simplest form because it does not require the reversal of medical interventions or legal transition. If an individual has transitioned socially and they choose to detransition, they can request that individuals refer to them utilizing the name and pronouns that they feel are most appropriate. They can adjust their attire, grooming methods, and mannerisms in a manner that they feel is appropriate based on their gender identity.

Social transition and/or social detransition is not, however, without risk. Individuals may experience harassment, discrimination, and even threats to safety in response to a decision to transition and/or detransition socially. Individuals also risk ostracism, alienation, and the potential loss of significant relationships due to transitioning or detransitioning. So from the outside looking in, it may seem as simple as a person deciding to wear a skirt and heels instead of dress slacks and oxfords, the truth is that the cost associated with that decision might be significant.

How Can Human Resources Support Someone Who Is in the Process of Social Transition?

Again, it is important that you be proactive. Do not wait until someone begins the process of social transition to make sure that your policies are affirming. The goals of the policies should be professionalism, as opposed to a specific gender expression.

- Make sure that you have clear policies in relation to the use of chosen names and pronouns.

- Make sure that you have clear and affirming policies around the use of toileting and changing facilities.

- Make sure that you have not unnecessarily gendered spaces in the workplace.

- Make sure that you have basic information available for people who do not understand or who desire additional information so that they do not rely on your transgender employee to get their questions answered.

- Make sure that your dress code and grooming standards are not unnecessarily gendered.

- Provide basic educational opportunities around LGBTQ+ sensitivity and transgender inclusion in the workplace.

- Consider providing training specific to allyship.

Having all of this information is a great first step, but now what does one do with this information? That is what we will discuss in the next chapter.

Part III

Workplace Dos and Don'ts

Chapter 7

Taking Initiative

If the previous chapters in this book have accomplished what they have set out to do, then you have learned some things about the transgender community that you did not know before beginning this book. But what good is all that knowledge if you don't put it into practice? People are eager to learn and so they seek out information, but that can't be where the journey ends. We should all aspire to utilize the information we learn in order to create safer spaces for all. So kudos to you for taking the first step in seeking information; now it's time for the next phase. There are things you can do with the information you've gathered that are meaningful and have the potential to affect change.

One of the first things you can do is commit to continue learning about the transgender community. The transgender community is changing with time. A younger demographic of individuals is identifying as transgender, and they have begun to take a deep dive into what it means to be transgender. That said, the information you receive in this book is just the beginning. I say that for two reasons. The information here is just the beginning because a lot more information about the transgender community is readily available. Also, this is only the beginning because the information in this book will likely change with time and advancements in medicine. Stated differently, as science progresses, so will the social implications of that science, and so you must stay abreast of new findings as they emerge.

The following chapters will answer one simple yet fundamental question: What do I do with all of this information? Let's dive right into the Dos and Don'ts!

Do accept responsibility for your education. The transgender community is not only rapidly growing but is changing and evolving with time. The onus is on you to care enough about this population not only to learn about it once, but to keep yourself informed as additional information becomes available. There may have been times in the past when information about the transgender community was not readily available, where speaking about the transgender community was in and of itself taboo. We have made a lot of progress, and there's a lot of information available about this community now, but you have to be willing to go and look for it. In so doing, please ensure that you are utilizing reliable sources of information. The transgender community can be a lightning-rod topic, so you must ensure that the information you are consuming is thoughtful, balanced, and as accurate as possible. When available, utilize peer-reviewed articles, or books that review the findings of peer-reviewed articles. Also, bear in mind sample size and lean toward obtaining information from studies or surveys with large sample sizes so that you are not making determinations about the transgender community based on a small number of opinions.

Don't rely on members of the transgender community to teach you about the transgender community. Members of historically marginalized groups often find themselves in a position where their organizations expect them to teach others about their marginalization. This is a particularly inappropriate ask, and it requires emotional labor on the part of someone who may already be contending with expectations that they do more than those around them to receive the same opportunities. Membership in a specific group does not automatically make you a subject matter expert. Moreover, being a subject matter expert does not automatically mean you want to be responsible for teaching others.

Do be proactive in seeking to better understand the transgender community. Your desire to create a safe space for the transgender community should not exclusively be the result of someone having gotten it wrong, of discrimination litigation, or even solely the result of learning that there is a transgender person on your staff, and you need to know how to handle that realization. It should be the case that you are seeking to create an environment that is safe and affirming for members of the transgender community even if, to your knowledge, there isn't any member of the transgender community employed at your organization. However, you should prioritize creating an empowering environment for this community in the same way that you are intentional in creating an empowering environment for other marginalized communities that enjoy less stigma, such as women.

Don't wait until someone complains about the environment before you seek to cultivate an affirming space. Do not wait until the law requires you to treat someone humanely before you seek to do so on your own. Do not wait for regulatory bodies to insist that you create an affirming space before you seek to create an affirming space on your own. Do not wait until you get it wrong before you seek to get it right.

Do put forth the effort to understand, at least on a rudimentary level, as many of the sexual orientations and gender identities as possible. If you know someone who is a sexual minority or gender minority, take the time to understand what that identity means to them. As the LGBTQ+ community continues to grow and expand, there will no doubt be additional identities added to what is already a beautiful and broad spectrum. Care enough to learn about these as they come to be so that you are better positioned to honor a person's identity when they share it with you.

Don't simply resign yourself to the fact that you're never going to be able to know all of the different sexual orientations or gender identities so you won't even try. All too often I hear people say something like "Oh, there's just so many letters. I can't keep up with this alphabet soup." They think those comments are harmless, but what this actually conveys to members of this community is that you don't think that their identity is important enough for you to put forth a good faith effort in trying to understand and learn about it.

Do reach out to your local LGBTQ+ organizations, not only to learn more about the community but to see how you might support the community in a meaningful way. National organizations are a wonderful source of information about the LGBTQ+ community, and they often provide amazing volunteer opportunities. There are likely individuals in your very own community who would very much appreciate your support and allyship, so whenever possible it is good to reach out to your local LGBTQ+ organizations to offer assistance and to see how you can be a value add.

Don't rely solely on books and articles to better understand the LGBTQ+ community. If it is possible, actually go and meet members of the community, speak to them, and get to know them; you will likely find out that they have more in common with you than you might think. Do not rely solely on the experiences of others to inform your perspective of this beautiful and vibrant community; instead, take it upon yourself to engage with the community. Most every LGBTQ+ organization not only allows but encourages the involvement of allies, so if you are an ally, get involved.

Do support LGBTQ+-specific causes. The amount of anti-LGBTQ+ legislation that is circulating right now is truly concerning to members of the LGBTQ+ community, and if you are an ally, it should be concerning to you too. Many organizations are working to push back against this legislation, but they need your help. So donate. Donate money, donate time, donate resources, donate your gifts and talents. Support in a tangible way.

Don't support causes that serve to either directly or indirectly undermine the LGBTQ+ community. You must understand the companies you do business with and their stance as it relates to the LGBTQ+ community. You must understand the stance that these companies have taken both privately and publicly as it relates to the LGBTQ+ community. One of the most impactful messages of support that you can send is to spend your money with companies that explicitly support the LGBTQ+ community and, just as importantly, not spend your money with companies that fail to explicitly pledge their support to the LGBTQ+ community.

Do be intentional in creating opportunities for advancement for transgender employees. As we discussed previously, transgender employees are often on the receiving end of discrimination. Unfortunately, unemployment and underemployment are common in the transgender community. One way that you can be of service is that if you are in a position to provide access to opportunities, you can be intentional in providing this access to individuals who are members of the transgender community. No one is asking for a handout. We're just asking for an opportunity to show we have what it takes. I have personally experienced discrimination directly associated with my being transgender. I had been moving up the ranks in the corporate world until I hit what I like to refer to as the "pink and blue ceiling." I reached a place where I could no longer advance, and there was no reasonable explanation. All of my performance reviews were exemplary. I had the skill set, the knowledge, and the work ethic but no matter what, I couldn't seem to get beyond the pink and blue ceiling, and it wasn't until after years of failed attempts that a recruiter finally shared with me the truth. He told me that the reason I wasn't being offered the position was because I was transgender, and the company was not ready to take that step. The recruiter thought I was amazing, and the person that I would have been reporting to directly thought I was amazing, but the higher-ups wouldn't allow for a transgender person to be hired into that position because it was a community-facing position and they didn't want a transgender person in that role.

I don't share this story to invoke sympathy, but to say that if there are individuals out there who will be explicit in their denial of opportunity to individuals who are transgender, then we need people out there who will be explicit in their determination to provide opportunities to people who are transgender. Will you be one of those people?

Don't assume that someone else is doing the work. Often people do not take the initiative because they assume that someone else will do so. "I would address that inappropriate comment, but I'm sure someone else will." "I would mentor her, but she seems like she already has support." "I would sponsor him, but he would probably prefer a sponsor who's a member of the LGBTQ+ community." These are examples of how we get it wrong and get in our own way. When we assume that someone would not benefit from our help because we believe they have access to help from other people, we rob them of the opportunity to learn and grow from working with us, and we rob ourselves of the opportunity to learn and grow from working with them. Don't assume that there's someone looking out for transgender employees. Unless that someone is you, you have no real way of knowing whether support is truly being rendered.

Do put forth a good faith effort instead of just setting it aside as something that's too difficult and therefore not worthy of even trying. Yes, you may falter, and you won't know everything. But there are lots of materials and resources available to help you better understand gender identity and sexual orientation, the difference between the two, and the most commonly endorsed identities, so if you

Taking Initiative

want to better understand, even on a very basic level, you can absolutely do that. Will it take work? Yes, but it's worth it, and so the question isn't, "Is the information available?" The question is, "Do you care to find it?"

You'll notice that this chapter was titled "Taking Initiative," not "Haphazardly Stumbling into the Possibility of Initiative." This word choice speaks to intentionality. You must set out to learn and grow and support others. You might stumble and fumble your way into a lesson or two, but you cannot stumble and fumble your way through this journey in its entirety. You must set the course, stay the course, and resolve yourself to help guide others through the course whenever possible.

Chapter 8

Using Gender Pronouns and Chosen Names

W'e're going to play a little game. I want you to take a moment and think about a coworker. This doesn't have to be someone that you're particularly close to, but it should be someone with whom you interact with on a relatively consistent basis. I would like you to tell a story about an interaction or an experience the two of you had together. But here's the catch: I want you to tell this story without using your coworker's name. Now, this isn't one of those moments where I provide instruction and you just keep reading. I really want you to take a moment and do what I'm asking you to do. You'll understand why in a moment. It doesn't have to be a long story; a story that lasts one to two minutes is just fine. Tell your story as if I'm sitting right there next to you and you're telling me all about what happened, but do not use this coworker's name. I'll wait.

OK, so you probably found that interesting but not terribly difficult because you had something else you could rely on, and if you're like most people, what you relied on were pronouns in the absence of the person's name. So let's take this game to the next level. I want you to tell me the same story as if I'm sitting right there next to you, but this time tell me the story without utilizing either the coworker's name or their pronouns. Make it as detailed as possible, and make sure you do not utilize the coworker's name or pronouns.

Now, if you're like most folks, that was much more difficult. And why is it so difficult to tell a story about a person without using their name and their pronouns? Because those are the two main identifiers we utilize when speaking about someone, and it is how we identify the subject of

123

our story. So now that we see how important a name and pronouns are in explaining, honoring, and giving voice to a person's experience, let's discuss how harmful it is when we do not get it right. The exercises you just engaged in highlight the fact that names and pronouns are how we show up in the world when we are explaining ourselves to others and when others are speaking about us and our experiences. A person's name is no small detail, nor is their choice of pronouns. They're very important details – ones that we should endeavor to get right.

In this chapter, we're going to explore the use of chosen names and gender pronouns. It is my hope that the previous exercise helped you to understand why they are so important. Now we'll look at the dos and don'ts of utilizing them in the workplace.

Do see the inherent value in utilizing a person's chosen name and pronouns. As individuals, we should be allowed to self-identify. We should decide how we would like to be seen by the world and those with whom we interact. When a person provides you with a chosen name, when they inform you of their pronouns, that is precisely what they are doing: determining how it is they will be referred to and, as an artifact of that, how it is that those around them will perceive them. Having the ability to utilize your chosen name and pronouns is a matter of self-determination. It is the ability to exercise your will when it comes to how you will be perceived. It is the sharing of your voice, an acknowledgment of self, a sign of intellectual and emotional freedom. It is perhaps one of the most basic forms of autonomy.

Don't minimize the importance of utilizing a person's chosen name and gender pronouns. Let's say, for example, that your name is Adam, but I consistently refer to you as Jeremy, and no matter how many times you correct me, I continue to refer to you as Jeremy. It would be really difficult for me to convince you that I see you and that I value you if I'm not willing to acknowledge you as you but instead insist on referring to you as someone other than who you know yourself to be. That is precisely what we do when we deadname someone – we communicate, even if inadvertently, that we do not see them and thus cannot truly value them and their contributions. The same can be said about utilizing the pronouns that a person has asked you to utilize. Imagine that your pronouns are he, him, and his, but every time I speak about you, I refer to you as she, her, and hers. What am I communicating to you by doing that? Am I communicating acceptance and affirmation? No, quite the contrary – I'm saying I do not see you the way that you see you, and I will not interact with you in a way that honors your sense of self, but I will instead prioritize my own personal comfort and my own perception over your sense of self and your truth.

Do encourage everyone to share their gender pronouns. When transgender individuals are the only people sharing their gender pronouns, what is supposed to create a safe and affirming environment turns into something that potentially outs a person. So instead of having only transgender people share their pronouns, it's best to encourage everyone to share their pronouns to normalize the practice. When cisgender people share their pronouns, it communicates to transgender people (and everyone, really) that they value gender identity and the ability of individuals to self-identify. So though it might seem inconsequential, sharing your pronouns is a great show of allyship.

Don't *require* that people share their gender pronouns. Not only does making the sharing of gender pronouns a requirement engender resentment in people who don't desire to, but it can also cause individuals to have to out themselves to their peers. Stated differently, you could inadvertently be placing someone in a position where they have to either misgender themselves or out themselves, and that's not a position that you should place anyone in, so you don't want to require that individuals share their pronouns. Still, you do want to encourage them to do so.

Do ask a person how they would like to be referred to. Would they like to be referred to as transgender? Would they prefer that you simply refer to them as the gender they identify with and leave the trans qualification off altogether?

Don't assume that a person wants you to refer to them with the qualifier of trans. For example, they might just want you to refer to them as a man as opposed to a trans man or a woman as opposed to a trans woman. Conversely, someone might find that their transgender identity is really important to them, and they might not feel comfortable with you leaving off transgender when referring to them. For example, they might only want you to refer to them as a trans man or a trans woman, so it's really important that you take the time to ask the question.

Do allow a person to utilize their chosen name and pronouns on all outward- and inward-facing documentation, communication, signage, and the like without requiring that they go through the process of legal transition. As discussed previously, there may be many reasons that an individual does not transition legally, and choosing not to transition legally should not prevent them from transitioning socially.

Don't make your transgender employees have to prove themselves to you. When you require that someone undergo legal transition, it is as if you are saying that legal transition is necessary for them to prove to you that they truly are transgender, and until they prove this to you, you will not honor it. Requiring legal transition to honor social transition is a form of gatekeeping, and it has the potential to disproportionately impact individuals of lower socioeconomic status who cannot afford the myriad fees associated with legal transition. Requiring medical transition as a prerequisite to honoring social transition is even worse, as not every individual wants to or has the means to transition medically. Putting this pressure on people is a dramatically unfair and unrealistic expectation.

Do self-correct when you get it wrong. If you deadname someone or misgender them, you can rest assured that they noticed. Something that I've seen quite a bit that I have found personally to be very uncomfortable and that others have shared with me is very uncomfortable as well is when a person deadnames or misgenders a person, and then just continues speaking as if it didn't just happen, as if they hope no one notices. The truth is that if you're dealing with someone who is transgender, it is highly unlikely that they won't notice if you deadname or misgender them. And as a general rule, I encourage people to self-correct when they notice that they have deadnamed or misgendered someone. It not only acknowledges that you have wronged them in some way, but it also reduces the likelihood of others hearing you and engaging in that same behavior.

Don't make a scene when you get it wrong. Self-correcting can be done quickly and respectfully without drawing a lot of attention and creating unnecessary discomfort on the part of the person who has been wronged. Stated differently, if you get it wrong, self-correct, apologize, and move on. Don't cause a scene.

There are two ways I see people cause a scene when they misgender or deadname someone, and I would like to encourage you not to engage in these behaviors. First is what I call the "apology monologue," when someone apologizes for far too long. Have you ever been in that situation? When someone apologizes, and apologizes some more, and keeps apologizing, you reach a point of diminishing returns. If you continue to apologize, all you're doing is causing more discomfort. Do not engage in this behavior.

I'll provide an example of an apology monologue to illustrate what I'm referring to. Let's say you are talking about me, and you misgender me. You utilize the pronouns she, her, and hers, and as soon as you do it, you catch yourself in an apology monologue that looks a little something like this. "Oh my goodness, I am so, so sorry, A.C. I cannot believe that I just misgendered you. It was not intentional, and I don't want you to think for a moment that it's because I don't view you as a man. Of course I view you as a man. I think that you are the manliest man that I've ever met, and I know that I said she, her, hers, but that was really more a reflection of just my, you know, not paying attention than it was of how I actually feel about you and how I see you in my heart. I mean, I guess what I'm trying to say is that I think that your masculinity is not at all in question. I apologize if my actions have caused you to feel as though I view you in a feminine light because that's not how I view you at all. I actually view you in a very masculine light. So I'm just really sorry because I don't want to make you uncomfortable by saying things that cause you to feel like you are not valued. Wait, what's that you say? It's OK? No, no, but it isn't OK. It isn't OK at all because it's important that I not engage in behaviors that cause you to feel less than. What's that? Just try harder next time? No, I mean, yeah, I mean, and I will. I promise that I will. I just want to make sure that I get it right this time because I recognize the impact that this might have had on you. . . ."

That, my friends, is an apology monologue, and it is unbelievably uncomfortable for all parties involved except for perhaps the person who's apologizing. I'm not quite clear on that one; I don't know if apologizing ad nauseam somehow is cathartic for the person doing it but, having been on the receiving end of many apology monologues, I do know that it is in no way, shape, or form cathartic for the person on the receiving end. I personally hate it and want

129

nothing more than for the exchange to stop. So please don't engage in this behavior.

The second misstep I see people make when they get it wrong is what I like to refer to as the "Woe Is Me," when a person apologizes for having gotten it wrong and starts speaking in a self-deprecating way. You don't want to engage in this behavior either because in most instances, the person who was originally wronged finds themselves in a position where they have to now come to the rescue of the person who wronged them because they are saying such negative things about themselves that the person that was wronged initially feels like they need to intervene on their behalf. So in that instance, not only have you wronged someone, but instead of righting the situation, you have somehow positioned yourself as the victim, and thus the person of focus, and that is exactly the opposite of what you should be doing.

Again, I'll provide an example to make sure that you understand so that you don't engage in this behavior. The Woe Is Me looks a little something like this. Let's assume the same situation that we utilized for the last example. "Oh, my goodness, A.C., I can't believe that I just did that. I am so stupid. And I know better and it doesn't make any sense that I would get this wrong. I've been practicing and everything when I'm not in your presence. I practice your pronouns. I practice your chosen name, and still when it matters most here I go again dropping the ball, messing it up again. No matter what I just can't seem to get it right – no, no, I mean, listen, I know you might not think that I'm a terrible person. Still, it's hard for me not to feel like a terrible person when I do things like this over and over and over again. I mean, the truth of the matter is what type of person am I that I can't seem to get out of my own way? I mean, yeah, sure, I treat you right in other ways. I just I need to get this particular way right. I just hate, hate, hate that I just can't ever seem to get this right. I'm sorry. I promise you I will do better next time. I mean, gosh, geez, here we go again."

You'll notice that scenario creates a situation in which the person who was actually wronged feels the need to intervene on your behalf and make you feel better, even though they are actually the person in need of some care and affirmation at that moment. That's not to say that you don't need a pep talk, but that shouldn't be the priority at that moment. So please don't engage in that behavior

There are few things more personal than our names and our gender pronouns. The sooner we realize that these are a matter of self-identification, the more quickly we can get to the work of valuing and affirming those around us. It is my hope that the exercises and examples in this chapter have helped you to understand more clearly why we must honor the names and the pronouns that individuals select for themselves.

Chapter 9

Respecting a Person's Individuality and Privacy

We place people, places, and things into categories in an attempt to better understand the world around us. In some instances this tendency is beneficial; it helps us streamline our intake of information, which is an important skill set to have given all of the stimuli that we come into contact with daily. However, this tendency can lead to gross misinterpretation, misunderstanding, and misappropriation of information. As much as we would love for things to be simple and to fit neatly into the boxes in our mind, the truth is that, all too often, that is not the case. Life is messy and people are nuanced, and when we lose sight of that, we're almost sure to engage in an unhelpful reliance on stereotypes.

How do we resist this tendency? We do it by intentionally pushing back whenever we find ourselves utilizing sweeping generalizations to describe people, places, or things. One might question if stereotypes serve as the very foundation of this book. I would submit to you that is not the case. Instead, if the reading of this book is landing how it was intended, what you are finding is that you are being asked at every juncture to consider multiple perspectives and ways of being. I am transgender, but I do not have a monopoly on the transgender experience. I am sharing my experience and the experience of others with whom I've worked and been in a relationship in hopes of broadening your perspective. The transgender community is not a monolith. We are beautifully diverse in our opinions, expectations, and desires. The value in this book is found not just in the provision of instruction and foundational knowledge, but it is also my hope that this book encourages open-mindedness that will serve you well, not just in working with transgender individuals but in relating to all people.

As we dive into this next section, I hope that you will keep all of this in mind and that I have effectively impressed upon you the heterogeneous nature of the transgender community. Now, let's dive into the dos and don'ts.

Do recognize that even though a person is a member of the transgender community, they are still very much an individual, and their opinions, feelings, perspectives, and convictions are their own. Understand that an individual may have belief systems you might not expect based on your stereotypes about the transgender community.

Don't expect a transgender person to speak for the entire transgender community. Do not expect one person to be able to represent the transgender community thoroughly or comprehensively. Do not treat the transgender community as if it were homogeneous or static. The transgender community is heterogeneous and dynamic.

Do understand that gender identity and existing on the gender binary does not necessarily mean that you subscribe to traditional gender roles. For example, you might meet a transgender man who does not subscribe to stereotypical male gender role expectations. He might enjoy things that are more stereotypically considered feminine, but that doesn't make him any less of a man. It just simply means that he's not limited to the confounds of gender role expectations. Said another way, the fact that someone knows they are a man doesn't mean that they're going to like only stereotypically masculine things.

The fact that someone knows that they are a woman doesn't mean that they're going to like only stereotypically feminine things. But just as a cisgender person can know their gender identity but not subject themselves unnecessarily to outdated, rigid gender norms, transgender individuals can do the same.

Don't expect overcompensation. That is to say, don't expect that a transgender man is going to engage in toxic masculinity or present in a hyper-masculine fashion because they identify as a man. You also should not expect that a transgender woman is going to be the epitome of all things feminine simply because she is a woman. We have to be careful not to position ourselves or our expectations such that we are expecting people to prove their gender identity to us by saying if you are a man, prove you are a man, and if you are a woman, prove you are a woman, nor should we expect them to do so by engaging in gendered expectations to the maximum degree. That is an unfair expectation, one that you should not place on transgender people in your life.

Do understand that people reserve the right to change their mind. The fact that someone feels a certain way today does not mean they have to feel that way indefinitely. For some people, sexual orientation and gender identity are more fluid than static and they may change over time or based on specific circumstances. It is important to understand that fidelity to a particular way of being is not a prerequisite for validity. You are who you say you are and if that changes over time, that is OK. I can use myself as an example. My understanding of my sexual orientation

Respecting a Person's Individuality and Privacy

changed with time, in part because I did not have the language to accurately describe my experience at first. So I originally identified as straight, and then once I came to understand what bisexuality was, I identified as bisexual. With time I found that my attraction was almost exclusively to women so I identified as a lesbian. But after deeper reflection and meeting some absolutely amazing men I felt pansexuality better described my orientation. But, again, I found that I had a strong preference for women, so I currently describe myself as omnisexual. But that too might change with time, and that is OK. It is important that we allow people space to self-identify.

Don't feel as though someone was disingenuous with you should the way they identify change over time. There are many reasons a person's view of themselves and their identity might change and it likely has nothing to do with you. So many factors inform a person's perspective of self, and if you assume that they intentionally withheld this information from you, you may be missing the mark. If someone who knew me when I identified as a woman were to speak to me now they would find that not only do I not identify as a lesbian but I no longer identify as a woman. Was I intentionally misleading people in my past? No. I just couldn't share what I didn't yet know.

Do respect the privacy of your transgender coworkers. Their personal life is just that – personal. It is never appropriate to inquire about an individual's medical past, present, or future. Likewise, it is never appropriate to inquire about an individual's sexual past, present, or future.

Don't expect your transgender employees or coworkers to share personal information about their transition, whether they are transitioning medically, legally, or socially. You should not anticipate that they are going to discuss their transition with you. Individuals will discuss what they are comfortable discussing when they are comfortable discussing it, and that should be OK.

Do understand that coming out as transgender can have real-world implications. It is a sad truth that individuals knowing that you're transgender has the potential to impact your employment, housing, and familial support negatively. Not everyone has the capacity or the desire to be out as a transgender person, and that should be OK. It should be respected and seen as valid. Transgender people don't owe outness to anyone. Being out as transgender can also increase the likelihood of a person experiencing harassment or even violence. So we shouldn't expect people to out themselves, and we should never out them.

Don't pressure people to pass. Not every transgender person is able to pass, And you are not more transgender if you are able to pass or less transgender if you are not.

Do hold space for differences of opinion, not just from your own but also from various members of the transgender community. Transgender folks come from all walks of life, representing all races, ethnicities, socioeconomic statuses, religious affiliations, varying educational attainment levels, and so on. So while being a member of the transgender community might be something they have in

Respecting a Person's Individuality and Privacy

common, there might be many things they do not have in common with one another.

Don't assume that because a person is a member of the transgender community, they might not themselves hold views that marginalize or oppress others. For example, a person can be transgender and racist, sexist, classist, and so on. Unfortunately, being a member of a marginalized community does not make you immune to the possibility of endorsing bigotry. That said, hatred needs to be addressed, no matter the source.

The truth of the matter is that we are all different. Humans are beautifully complex, and this complexity is found in all people groups, the transgender community included. You must balance seeking to learn about the community overall and remembering that individual lived experiences will always hold just as much weight as collective experiences.

Chapter 10

Establishing Policies, Practices, and Procedures

Most adults spend a significant portion of their waking hours at work. We spend so much time at work that not working in a supportive and affirming environment is a quality-of-life issue. Almost every adult I know works 40 or more hours a week, which doesn't include the time spent preparing for or decompressing from work. Many of us spend more time at work than we do with our families. Anything that takes up that much of our time is worth examining in detail. As we take a closer look at what work environments are like for members of the transgender community, ask yourself a few questions:

- Is my work environment safe for transgender employees? Think beyond physical safety and explore within yourself whether you think your work environment is safe from an emotional and psychological standpoint for members of the transgender community.

- Have we been active in creating an affirming space specifically for members of the transgender community, or are we wholly reliant on the absence of potentially harmful behaviors?

- Do we have clear and robust policies regarding the treatment of transgender individuals, or are we relying entirely on a generic civility policy? We must realize that both action and inaction send very clear messages.

There are some matters in which you simply cannot be neutral. You must take a stand, and failure to take a stand is a stand in and of itself. Let's jump into the dos and don'ts.

Do ensure that you have robust policies and procedures around the intentional use of a person's given name, otherwise known as their deadname, despite being aware of their chosen name, as well as the intentional use of gender pronouns consistent with the gender associated with the sex that they were assigned at birth when aware that other gender pronouns are the requested pronouns. It is very important that deadnaming and misgendering, when done intentionally, be viewed as harassment and/or bullying and that they be covered in any zero-tolerance policies that you have around harassment or bullying.

Don't assume that you know how a person would like you to address situations in which you see them being deadnamed or misgendered. Unless you actually ask them for guidance, you can't be sure what their wants and needs are. Some individuals will want you to correct someone if they deadname or misgender them, and others would prefer that you act as though you did not hear it at all. Some will prefer that you address it in real time, even if it is in their presence. Others will prefer that you wait until you are no longer in their presence and address it privately with the person who misgendered them. Some would like you to correct someone who misgendered them even if it happens not in their presence. Others would prefer that you ignore it if it happens outside of their presence.

There are an unlimited number of desired reactions and responses to deadnaming and misgendering, so it's really important that you actually ask a person what it is that they would desire for you to do and that you honor whatever is requested. You do not want to create a situation that makes the transgender person more uncomfortable or causes them to be further ostracized, harassed, or bullied. Also, understand that a person's desire might change with time, and so the fact that they currently would like for you to correct someone if they misgender them does not mean that they will feel that way in the future, and it should be OK for that to change as many times and as often as necessary.

Also, understand that a person might desire for you to address it one way with someone they know and another way with someone they do not know. For example, if I am interacting with someone with whom I know I'm going to have continued or repeated interactions and they misgender me or deadname me, I will correct them because I don't want to continue to have that experience over and over again. But suppose I'm interacting with someone I will likely never see again (such as a server in a restaurant out of town). In that case, in most instances I will not correct them because correcting individuals is emotionally taxing for me. I don't see it as particularly valuable if I am not going to see them again. But even that is nuanced because if it's someone who engages in frequent niceties – like saying "ma'am," "sir," or "ladies or gentlemen" – and I'm going to have to hear it repeatedly even in just that one sitting, then I might correct them because I don't want to be called "ma'am" 10 to 15 times while I'm trying to enjoy my dinner. The matter is nuanced, and unless you ask me what I desire, you won't know. The fact that I desire one response in this situation in this environment doesn't necessarily mean that I will desire the same response in a different situation in a different environment.

Also, safety should be taken into consideration. In some environments a person might feel like it's safe to correct individuals who misgender or deadname them, and in other environments they might feel like this actually compromises their safety. The extent to which a person is in a position of authority might impact whether they would like a person to be corrected. Correcting your coworker is different than correcting your supervisor, which is different than correcting a subordinate, and so all of those situations might call for different responses. This is why it's important that we actually give people an opportunity to make us aware of what they desire and that we extend grace and space for them to change their mind as often as is necessary for them to maintain a level of comfort in the work environment.

Obviously, you can't ask your transgender colleague for a detailed spreadsheet of every reaction you should have for every circumstance. But asking for guidance can help you understand what their most important desires are on this matter, and you can let them know that you're supportive if they ever want to share any further or updated guidance on this.

Do provide various opportunities for your employees to learn about the LGBTQ+ community. This can include training, seminars, workshops, fireside chats, keynotes, and e-learning modules; there are so many ways to present employees with information about the LGBTQ+ community that there really is no excuse for not ensuring that your employees are well informed. Many organizations make their LGBTQ+ training voluntary. To do so is fine, but if you're going to make LGBTQ+ sensitivity voluntary, it is really important that you make explicit mention of members of the LGBTQ+ community in your no harassment, zero bullying, zero tolerance trainings that are mandatory. Employees really should be expected to come into contact with information about this community and to understand that harassment and/or bullying of members of this community will not be tolerated.

Don't limit your training opportunities as they relate to the transgender community to a few sentences in a larger presentation about the LGBTQ+ community more generally. The desire might be there to do this because you feel people will be more receptive to generalized training, but you must remember that the transgender community is experiencing unique stressors and is the focus of much anti-trans rhetoric, anti-trans legislation, and anti-trans policies and procedures. Because of this, you must be explicit in your support of the transgender community and recognize, support and affirm them even outside of conversations about the LGBTQ+ community in general.

Do be intentional in the allocation of resources to support the LGBTQ+ community in general and the transgender community more specifically. Ensure that your employees have access to and understand widely accepted best practices regarding the subject of including transgender individuals in the workplace. Make sure that there is foundational or rudimentary information available about the transgender community so that an individual who perhaps is just becoming acquainted with the transgender community has a place to go to learn the basics.

Don't allow a perceived sense that there are only a few LGBTQ+ employees or there are only a few transgender employees to be the reason that you do not allocate appropriate resources. It's important to remember that you cannot accurately assess a person's gender identity without relying upon self-identification. So the fact that you don't see anyone you believe is transgender doesn't mean that there are no transgender employees. The fact that a person has not identified or outed themselves to you doesn't mean that they do not exist, and even if there are only a couple of transgender employees, it's still important that you do everything possible to create a safe environment for them. Even if you have no employees who are transgender, to your knowledge, it is still important for your employees to learn about the community and how best to create space and hold space for them. That way, when a transgender person does come into contact with you or a member of your organization, they're likely to be affirmed and supported as opposed to harmed in some way.

Do ensure that your employees have the ability to create and sustain a resource group specific to the LGBTQ+ community should they desire to do so. The reason I said "create and sustain" is because resource groups require proper funding by the greater organization. It's important that you ensure that your LGBTQ+-specific resource group is fully funded and that they have a budget robust enough to bring in outside experts; otherwise, you'll find that what you are essentially doing is relying on your employees to educate one another and to educate you but doing it underneath the umbrella of a resource group, which is an unfair expectation. You should also understand that being the chair or co-chair of an employee resource group is time-consuming and entails additional work. That additional work and time should be compensated, whether that means compensating employees for a certain number of hours a month that they can dedicate specifically to running the resource group, or providing them a stipend of some sort. It's important that you acknowledge the emotional labor and the additional work involved in being the chair or co-chair of a resource group and that you compensate them for doing so. It is also important that your LGBTQ+ resource group have an executive sponsor – a member of the executive team who sponsors this specific group. They don't have to be a member of the LGBTQ+ community, but at the very least they do need to be an ally. This will allow the LGBTQ+ resource group to have a voice in the room at the highest levels, which is very important.

Don't require your LGBTQ+ resource group to fundraise its own money. It is important that you show support for this group by providing them with adequate funding. Do not require LGBTQ+ employees to have to try to figure out who else is in the community and would like to connect on that basis. That is precisely what you require of your LGBTQ+ employees when you fail to make an LGBTQ+-specific resource group available. Having them find one another requires that they rely on stereotypes, assumptions, or potentially inappropriate questions to identify one another; this can be completely avoided when the organization ensures that there is a safe space to meet other LGBTQ+ individuals. One phenomenal example of that is an employee resource group.

Do allow people to use whatever bathroom, locker room, or changing facility they feel comfortable with. Do recognize that gender identity and gender expression are not synonymous. That said, a person might choose to use a restroom that appears to be inconsistent with their gender expression. It is important that you not take that to mean that they are utilizing a restroom inconsistent with their gender identity. There can be many reasons why a person's gender identity and gender expression don't align, and so again, what's most appropriate is to allow people to choose what they are most comfortable doing and grant them the space to do just that.

Don't create single stalls or separate restrooms specifically for transgender employees to use. Transgender employees should be able to utilize the restroom consistent with their gender identity. When you create a restroom that is separate and distinct from the other restrooms and you identify it as the restroom that a transgender person should use, you're really engaging in ostracization and othering. Instead, if you would like to have a separate and distinct restroom, you should make that restroom available for anyone who feels more comfortable in a separate and distinct restroom. Stated differently, the transgender person should be able to go to whatever restroom they feel comfortable using just like anyone else can, and if there's someone who is not comfortable using a restroom that a transgender person might also use, they might decide that they would prefer to utilize the single-stall separate restroom so that they are not in the restroom with a transgender employee.

Do acknowledge nationally and internationally recognized days of observance. For example, it is important that your organization recognizes certain days of commemoration, such as Transgender Awareness Week, Transgender Day of Visibility, Transgender Day of Remembrance, and the International Day against Homophobia, Biphobia, and Transphobia.

Don't acknowledge Pride month generally without acknowledging specific dates of commemoration. This may be as simple as acknowledging a date of commemoration by posting on social media as a company or facilitating a training or a fireside chat on one of the days of commemoration.

Do take stock of yourself and your individual behavior. Understand that no one is immune from making mistakes, engaging in microaggressions, perpetuating stigma, and the like, so we must take a very close and honest look at ourselves to make sure that our behavior isn't further jeopardizing members of the transgender community. Do people know that they can come and speak to you about their gender identity? Are you a safe space for that conversation? Do individuals know that they can come to you and ask questions to gain a better understanding of the community? Are you able to answer questions, and if not, are you able to at least point them in the right direction? Do you know how people in your organization wish to be addressed? Do you know what pronouns they utilize? What names they have chosen for themselves? Do you know how transgender individuals in your organization would like for you to respond if you hear someone misgendering them either in or out of their presence? Do you know what your organization's policies are around deadnaming and misgendering, and if they aren't robust enough, have you made that known to individuals who have the ability to change them? Are you aware of the relevant legislation in your state regarding the transgender community? Are you aware of what resources are available in your community for members of the transgender community? And if the answer to these questions is no, then perhaps the most important question of all is, do you care enough to find out?

Don't dismiss this as being someone else's responsibility. You must be intentional in creating a safe work environment for your transgender employees, colleagues, and customers. The above shift in mindset and behaviors is an excellent way to be a value-add.

Do extend yourself grace. You are not going to get it right 100% of the time. There will be times that you make mistakes and times that you falter. You should expect this to happen, and when it does, quickly and authentically apologize and do better. If you enter this journey expecting that you're going to get it right all of the time, you are setting yourself up for failure. Even the most well-intentioned people are fallible. Making a mistake doesn't make you a bad person. It simply makes you human. But it is important that we not excuse our behavior so much so that we are not truly putting forth a good-faith effort. If you notice that you have a propensity to get certain things wrong, then the onus is on you to put mechanisms in place that will lessen the likelihood of that error. That is to say, it is unacceptable to continue to err without improvement. There is immense value in learning how to appropriately and respectfully talk to, with, and about the transgender community. And I salute you for taking the time to begin the process of educating yourself.

We have discussed what you should do with the information you have received. But this book is not meant to be exhaustive, and as such you may very well have some questions that remain unanswered. We will tackle that reality in the next chapter.

Part IV

Building on This Foundation

Chapter 11

What If My Question Wasn't Answered?

I hope you have learned a great deal in reading this book, and not just about the transgender community from a demographic standpoint or the types of transition members of the transgender community may choose to engage in. I hope you've also learned ways to support and affirm transgender people, particularly those in the workplace. While this book has a great deal of information, it is not all-encompassing. I've tried to answer the most common questions I am presented with, and I've tried to provide foundational understanding. I'm sure there are still many questions that remain unanswered. So what do you do if you still have a question that has not been answered by the material presented in this book? That's actually a question in and of itself, and I'd like to answer it.

Curiosity

Generally speaking, it's great to be curious. Many work environments encourage curiosity, and depending on your field of work it might even be an essential part of your daily life. It is a characteristic often present in high performers. But unfettered curiosity can be problematic. Some things are simply none of your business. Thus we cannot utilize curiosity as the meterstick by which we determine if we should ask someone a question. If you find yourself curious about aspects of your transgender colleague's life, pause before asking a question and ascertain whether it's actually an appropriate question. To determine this, ask yourself the following questions:

- "Does the answer to this question directly impact my work?" If the answer is no, you should not ask the question.

- "Would I ask this question to anyone else on the team?" If the answer is no, you should not ask the question.

- "Would I ask my boss this question?" If the answer is no, you should not ask the question.

- "Might this question make the person on the receiving end uncomfortable?" If the answer is yes, you should not ask the question.

- "Does their answer to this question directly impact their ability to complete their work?" If the answer is no, you should not ask the question.

- This last question might sting a little, but I'm going to propose it anyway. Ask yourself, "Am I just being nosey?" If the answer to that question is yes, then you should not ask the question.

I'm not saying there's anything wrong with being curious, but asking someone a personal question to curb your curiosity is not OK. So what do you do with this curiosity? How do you get answers if not by asking your coworker? Great question. We'll talk about that next.

Doing Your Own Research

So let's say you have a question, but you have thought about it and you realize that it's really just rooted in curiosity. What should you do next? Well, what you should not do is ask your coworker. You should try to find the information on your own from a reliable source. I cannot stress enough the importance of ensuring it is a reliable source. There are a lot of people with a lot of opinions, and you don't want to rely on the opinions of individuals to source your information. You want to utilize peer-reviewed articles and research to further your understanding of this and any other community. Chances are you're not the first person to have this question. If you utilize your resources, you can find literature that not only answers your question but provides the foundational understanding necessary to be able to meaningfully apply the information that you find.

You want to look out for a couple of things, though. Watch out for information that is clearly biased or leaning in one direction. All aspects of life have both positive and negative attributes, so if you come across literature that seeks to paint the transgender community as wholly positive or wholly negative, it's not likely a reliable source of information. Likewise, the literature around this community is still developing and always will be, so if you come across something that presents itself as the be-all and end-all in terms of information about transgender individuals, it's likely not a reputable source of information. I also caution against accepting whole cloth the ideas or perspectives of one person; make sure that you are sourcing your information from research with robust sample sizes so you know that what you are learning is not rooted in the lived experience of one individual. It's also imperative that you go back periodically to find out what the new literature is on this topic because as the demographic shifts, as the population size grows, as legislation is passed, as large corporations offer support or pull back support, as celebrities and influencers speak out, the overall standing of the community within the zeitgeist of the time will shift. So it's important that you're not utilizing our understanding of the community from times past to inform your present decisions and work.

Altruistic or Egoistic?

Another thing to consider when trying to determine if you should ask a question of a transgender colleague is whether a question is altruistic or egoistic. Does asking this question somehow serve to benefit the transgender person? Will the answer to this question allow you to create a safer and more affirming space for them? Will the answer allow you to make a more productive and positive work environment for them? Will it afford them opportunities that they wouldn't have otherwise? What is in it for them? If you can't think of straightforward ways that this question benefits them, then you should not ask it. If the only purpose it serves is to put things into clear perspective for you, there are other ways you can approach obtaining that information. What I'm getting at here is the underlying question of whether you are asking this question to benefit them or to benefit you. If the answer is "I am asking this question to benefit me," then you should not ask the question.

Nature of the Relationship

Next, consider the nature of your relationship with this person. Is this question appropriate based on the nature of that relationship? Is it relevant and in keeping with that relationship? If you are my coworker, I have absolutely no need to understand your sex life, your genitalia, your romantic inclinations, your childhood trauma, your levels of familial acceptance, and so on. If we are coworkers, I don't really need to know anything about you outside of what directly impacts our work together. So you must ask yourself, what is the nature of my relationship with this person? Are we friends, are we simply coworkers, are we colleagues, are we associates? Once you have answered that question honestly, how appropriate is it for you to ask someone this particular question based on the nature of your relationship?

You must also take into consideration whether there is any power differential in your relationship. Is this a subordinate? Is this a peer? Is this a supervisor? Might a person feel like they have to answer your question because of the power differential? And bear in mind that a power differential doesn't exist only by way of professional seniority; there are other ways in which power can exist and be exerted. For example, any aspect of privilege that you have can be exerted as power, and a person of a marginalized background might feel the presence of that power even if it's not your intention to wield it. If you are White and I am Black and you ask me a question, I might feel I have to answer your question. If you are a man and I am a woman and you ask me a question, I might feel I have to answer your question. If you are heterosexual and I am queer and you ask me a question, I might feel I have to answer that question. If you are Christian and I am Muslim and you ask me a question, I might feel as though I have to answer that question. If you are cisgender and I am transgender and you ask me a question, I might feel I have to answer that question. You might not be wielding power intentionally, but even without conscious intent, that doesn't mean a power differential is not present and is not felt. So before you ask a question, ask yourself, is there any element of privilege that might cause this person to feel as though they have to answer me, even though they aren't comfortable doing so? If the answer to that question is yes, you should not ask the question.

Safety

It's important to understand that when a person outs themselves as transgender or gender nonconforming, this can be potentially dangerous. The danger can present itself in many ways. A person's physical safety can be at risk because, sadly, there are individuals who have such strong negative feelings about the transgender community that they will actually seek to do them physical harm. There are also individuals who will not physically harm a person but will shun them, ostracize them, gossip about them, or otherwise make their life miserable, and so even in instances where physical safety is not a concern, a person might need to be concerned about emotional or psychological safety. Additionally, a person can be at risk of losing their employment or losing access to opportunities for advancement because they are outed as transgender. It's also the case that a person's housing can be compromised by individuals finding out that they're transgender.

So how is this relevant to the workplace? In the workplace, if you ask someone a question for which the answer could potentially put them in harm's way, it is important that you know with absolute certainty that you're able to protect them. If you cannot say without a shadow of a doubt that you can protect this person from experiencing discrimination as a result of their gender identity, then you should not ask them questions that could potentially put them at risk. And even if you could somehow know that you could protect them from discrimination, it is not up to you to decide for them to endure discrimination on your account. So the issues goes beyond whether you can protect them if they answer your question, but it also involves you considering, "Is answering my question going to place them in harm's way?" If the answer to that question is yes, then it is not a fair question to ask.

The Expected End

It's important to understand the why behind asking a question. What is your goal? What is the expected end? Are you asking this question so that you can better understand the person? Are you asking so that you can better understand what motivates them? Are you asking so that you can support them in their current efforts?

Once you have identified the why behind the question, you can begin to identify a more appropriate way to achieve that end. For example, if the goal is to get to know the person better, there are many ways you can get to know someone that have absolutely nothing to do with their gender identity. You don't need to know how old they were when they realized they were transgender or whether they identify on the gender binary or anything like that in order to get to know them better. You can always ask something benign, not particularly personal or potentially uncomfortable. For example, you might ask what their hobbies or interests are, or if they like to read, you could ask about their favorite book or their favorite author. If you're trying to get to know someone better, think about ways you can learn about them that don't require the answering of deeply personal questions.

If the goal is to learn how to better support them, it's best to ask that question directly. What do you need from me at this moment? How can I better support you? What can I do to be a value add? That's much better than asking probing questions in hopes of somehow linking the information together in a meaningful way so that you can utilize what you have learned to support them.

What is the expected end? What are you trying to accomplish by asking this particular question? Once you have identified that, you can find another way to meet that need. If, upon reflection, you realize that you can't really identify the expected end, that means you don't really have a reason to be asking, and therefore you should not be asking the question.

Asking the Question

Suppose you've gone through all of the previous steps and have determined, miraculously, that your question is, in fact, appropriate and necessary. In that case, the question now becomes, how do you ask? So let's talk about how you go about asking the question if it is, in fact, appropriate to ask.

Privacy

If you're going to ask someone a question about their experience as a transgender person, it's important that you ask them privately. Even if a person is comfortable answering your question, they might not be comfortable sharing this information with a group of people, so it's best not to ask questions of this sort in the presence of others. Having said that, I would caution you against asking the question at all because while, on the one hand, it is a great idea to ask privately so as not to embarrass someone, on the other hand, it can increase the likelihood that a person feels uncomfortable, almost as if you're asking privately adds an additional layer of "ick" to the asking of the question. So it's probably best not to ask the question at all. But if you're going to ask the question you don't really want to ask in front of a group of people, and you're going to ask privately, you probably want to preface it with some explanation as to why you're asking privately and not in the presence of others.

Opt-Out

It needs to be abundantly clear that a person can choose not to answer your question. You do not want to assume that they know this; instead, you should state this expressly. You might say something like, "You don't have to answer this question if you don't want to, but I was wondering. . ." or "Feel free to tell me that this is none of my business, but. . ." Having said that, if you have to preface a question with one of those two statements, you probably shouldn't be asking it in the first place. But if you insist on asking, you should preface it with an opt-out clause.

What If My Question Wasn't Answered?

Acknowledgment of Power Differential

You must acknowledge the power differential in the relationship if there is one. Make it clear that you understand that there's a power differential and that it is important to you that they know that they do not have to answer your question despite this power differential. Naming the power differential might seem like an uncomfortable thing to do because, well, it's an uncomfortable thing to do. But that is probably more a testament to the fact that you shouldn't be asking the question than to the fact that you shouldn't be clearly stating the difference in power.

Work-Related Questions Only

If you're going to ask a question, it really should be the case that you're only asking questions where the answer directly impacts the work that the two of you do together. If the answer does not directly impact the work that you or the other person does, then you should not be asking that question. Most questions about a transgender person's lived experience are not actually going to be work-related, and therefore should not be asked. If the question is only related to your work indirectly or peripherally, then you should not be asking the question. We should only ask questions that are directly related to the work.

Subject Matter Expert

Being a member of a specific group does not necessarily make you a subject matter expert as it relates to that group. You should not ask a transgender person to answer questions on behalf of the entire transgender community.

An individual is just that – an individual – and it's not fair to place the burden of representation on someone who has not volunteered to carry that burden. There are individuals out there who are actually subject matter experts, and it's best to ask them your questions, as opposed to asking your coworkers or colleagues.

Additionally, let's say your coworker actually is a subject matter expert, for whatever reason. That does happen from time to time. But it's important to remember that being a subject matter expert does not mean that you necessarily want to be the person to educate on that subject in that particular setting. So we should not assume, just because a person has the knowledge, that they are comfortable or that they desire to share their knowledge in the workplace.

It's also important to realize that just as your transgender coworker might be a subject matter expert, they could very well be a complete novice and know very little about the community, and that should be OK because you shouldn't be relying upon them to help you learn. There are people who do this work and answer these questions for a living, so save your questions for us. That's what we're here for.

Putting It All Together

Now let's say you have truly checked every box. By that I mean all of the following:

- The question is not being fueled simply by curiosity.
- You've done your own research but still can't find the answer, and you're asking for purely altruistic reasons.

- The nature of your relationship supports asking such a personal question.

- You can ensure their safety if they answer your question.

- The expected result of answering the question is something that is actually beneficial to the other person.

- You are able to ask them privately, and you have tailored the question in a way that ensures the ability to opt out.

- You have acknowledged the power differential and made sure that you expressly speak to that in asking the question.

- It is a work-related question.

- The person you're asking is not only a subject matter expert but has made it clear to you that they desire to utilize their expertise to answer personal questions in a work environment.

If you can say yes to all of that, then go ahead and ask the question.

If the above checklist seems like a bit much, it's because it is meant to be a bit much. There honestly are very few circumstances in which it is appropriate to ask someone about their personal life. The process by which we decide whether to ask potentially intrusive questions should be rigorous. We should err on the side of not asking, not on the side of satisfying our curiosities. And that is what I hope to have conveyed in this chapter.

Chapter 12

Conclusion

We have covered a lot of information in this book and it's time to wrap things up. As I reflected on the best way to do so, I found myself thinking perhaps we should do a bit of a recap. I can't hit every point, but I want to revisit some of the highlights and make sure you know where in the book to find information concerning specific areas if you need clarification.

Chapter 1, "Getting to Know the Transgender Community"

We discussed several things in Chapter 1. It's important that you remember the difference between sex assigned at birth and gender identity. When we confuse these two concepts, we make faulty assumptions and inaccurate generalizations. The sex you were assigned at birth relies almost exclusively on the medical professional's exclamation after seeing your genitals for the first time. Your gender identity is a matter of self-identification. It is the deep internal sense of gender. It is whether you feel like a boy, a girl, a combination of the two, a third gender, or perhaps have no sense of gender at all. Gender identity is not how someone else describes you based on societal norms, but how you describe yourself based on your own sense of identity.

It's also important that you remember the distinction between transgender and cisgender. If your gender identity aligns with the sex that you were assigned at birth, then you are considered cisgender. If your gender identity does not align with the sex that you were assigned at birth, then you are considered transgender. Transgender is an umbrella term, and it's important to recall that some individuals who are transgender do not feel like they fit exclusively within the gender binary; we refer to those individuals as nonbinary.

When it comes to numbers, you'll recall that there are an estimated 1.3 million to 2 million transgender adults in the United States alone. Additionally, there are an estimated 300,000 youth ages 13 to 17 who identify as transgender in the United States. When we take a closer look at demographics, we find that the racial makeup of the transgender community is quite similar to the racial makeup of the United States in general. As it relates to age, the age of transgender individuals, at least in the United States Transgender Survey, tended to skew young. That is to say that individuals who identified as transgender seem to be younger in age. I'll reiterate that I don't believe that is an artifact of there being more transgender people now than there were in previous generations as much as it is an artifact of individuals being more comfortable identifying themselves as transgender and sharing that reality with others.

When considering geographical location, we find that transgender individuals are more likely to live in the western portion of the United States than they are to live in the southern portion of the United States. Those findings aren't particularly surprising because the southern part of the United States has a tendency to lean more conservative than the West, so individuals may be less likely to come out as transgender if they live in the South, or they might be more likely to move away from the South and relocate to the West if they are transgender.

When it comes to languages spoken in the home, transgender individuals are more likely to live in homes where English is the only language spoken than are their cisgender counterparts. This might not mean anything at all, but it might also be an artifact of deeply rooted cultural expectations in that Western countries might be more accepting of the transgender community than other countries. I don't know this to be true, but it's worth exploring.

When considering faith, we find that 63% of members of the transgender community report having some connection to religion or spirituality. Transgender individuals tend to be more highly educated than their cisgender counterparts. Unfortunately, this fact does not necessarily equate to economic standing. Even though transgender individuals tend to have more education than cisgender individuals, they also tend to experience more unemployment and underemployment than their cisgender counterparts do. Strikingly, a transgender person is significantly more likely to live beneath the poverty line than their cisgender counterparts. I am of the belief that this is a direct result of discrimination in hiring practices as well as a lack of opportunities for advancement in the workforce.

Transgender persons are significantly more likely to have a disability than their cisgender counterparts. Transgender individuals are more likely to be citizens by birth than the general population. Again, this might be an artifact of transgender individuals who are born in the United States feeling more comfortable sharing that they are transgender than individuals who were born outside of the United States and are perhaps more engrossed in other cultures.

When it comes to sexual orientation, many people assume incorrectly that transgender people are most likely to be straight. This is an assumption that makes sense, particularly if you are comparing transgender people to the general population, in which the lion's share of people identify as straight. But that is not the case for the transgender community. Only 15% of the transgender community identify as straight, whereas 21% of the transgender community identify as queer, 18% identify as pansexual, and 16% identify as gay.

Transgender people are less likely than the general population to be married. It is unclear if transgender individuals are less likely to get married or if this discrepancy is an artifact of relationships coming to an end when a spouse or partner finds out that you are, in fact, transgender. I say this because research indicates that 27% of the transgender community reported that a partner ended their relationship either solely or partly because they were transgender. Sadly, 10% of the time it was solely because they were transgender. And this tendency seems to be more pronounced for transgender women in that 18% of transgender women report the ending of a relationship solely because they are transgender, as opposed to 9% of transgender men. Additionally, 21% of transgender individuals report losing their relationship with their children either permanently or temporarily when their children find out that they're transgender. Again, this impacts transgender women at a much higher rate than it does transgender men.

As we have discussed, being out as transgender often has profound consequences when it relates to your family of origin; 26% of individuals in the transgender community who are out to their immediate family reported that at least one family member either stopped speaking to them or ended the relationship with them altogether. Worse still, 10% of transgender individuals report that they experienced violence toward them by a family member. Violence, however, is not the only threat, as 8% of members of the transgender community who are out to their family are kicked out of the house because they are transgender. And transgender individuals who are kicked out of the house are more likely to live in poverty and have lower incomes overall. They are three times more likely to have engaged in sex work, and 74% experienced homelessness. They are more than twice as likely to be living with HIV, are at significant risk of attempting suicide, and have an increased risk of experiencing psychological distress. But I don't want you to remember only the trauma. The good news is that not all members of the transgender community who are out to their family experience violence or rejection; 82% of them report having experienced some level of support from at least one family member. Some examples of familial support include telling a transgender person that they support them or respect them; using their chosen name; using the correct pronouns; standing up for them; doing research to try to learn how to support them best; giving money to help in their transition; and helping with changing their name and/or gender on ID documents.

Thirty-nine percent of transgender individuals report currently experiencing serious psychological distress, which is significantly higher than the 5% of the general population that reports the same. Notably, suicidality is a significant concern when it comes to the transgender community. Transgender individuals are nearly 10 times more likely than members of the general population to attempt suicide at some point. Whereas 4.6% of members of the general population have attempted suicide at some point in their life, 40% of members of the transgender community have attempted suicide at some point in their life.

Finally, let's discuss detransitioning, which is when a member of the transgender community goes back to living as the sex they were assigned at birth. I would like to remind you that this is not a common phenomenon, despite the frequency with which it is discussed by opponents of gender-affirming care. Only 8% of individuals in the transgender community reported detransitioning. Of that 8%, the majority only detransitioned temporarily, with more than 60% going on ultimately to live their lives in a manner consistent with their gender identity as opposed to the sex they were assigned at birth.

Chapter 2, "Experiences in the Workplace"

In Chapter 2, we discussed the experiences of transgender individuals in the workplace. Unfortunately, many transgender individuals experience discrimination in the workplace after having often jumped through many hoops to find suitable employment in the first place. As for being out as transgender, data has shown that 49% of transgender individuals currently working report that they are not out as transgender to any of their bosses or supervisors. In addition to not being out to bosses and supervisors, you find a similar dynamic when it comes to being out to any coworker at all, with 42% of transgender individuals reporting that they're not out to anyone in the workplace, period. You might wonder if such caution is warranted. Sadly, the numbers support the need for discretion, with 39% of those who experienced not being hired in the past year reporting that they were not hired because of their gender identity or expression; 49% reported that their gender identity or expression was the reason they were not promoted, and 43% reported that their gender identity or expression was the reason they were terminated or made to resign. What's more, individuals in the transgender community often experience this discriminatory behavior and attempt to navigate it on their own without any assistance, with the lion's share not reporting the discrimination at all. This is important for us to bear in mind as we seek to ascertain the safety of our work environments. Stated differently, we cannot take the absence of filed complaints or official grievances to mean that discriminatory behavior is not taking place because we know that this particular population will likely not report the wrongdoings.

All things considered, it comes as no surprise that many transgender individuals go to great lengths to avoid experiencing discrimination in the workplace, with 53% hiding their gender identity, 47% not asking their employer to use the appropriate pronouns, 26% delaying their gender transition, 26% staying in a job that they would have preferred to leave, 25% hiding that they had already transitioned their gender, 24% keeping a job for which they were overqualified, 15% quitting their job, 30% not seeking a promotion or a raise, 6% requesting or transferring to a different position or department, and 77% engaging in one or more of the behaviors just mentioned.

It's important to recall that the very act of finding employment can be difficult for members of the transgender community. Transgender individuals are often left to hide who they truly are in order to be given an opportunity to work at all, with 50% of transgender individuals reporting that they could not be their full authentic selves during the interview process. And even if they manage to get hired, transgender employees often find themselves relegated to entry-level positions and not provided with the opportunity to excel and advance within the workplace.

Chapters 3 Through 6, "Core Questions About Transition"

In Chapter 3, we discussed transition. You'll recall that there are three widely recognized forms of transition in the transgender community: social, medical, and legal. Individuals may transition in all, some, or none of these ways. Transitioning is not a prerequisite for transgender identification. That is to say, a person might opt out of transitioning in any way, shape, or form, and their identification as transgender is just as valid as someone who has transitioned in all three ways. There are many reasons that an individual might decide not to transition, as we discussed in Chapter 3, including lack of access, lack of means, lack of desire, societal expectations, fear for their safety, religious beliefs, and many other reasons.

Chapter 3 provides a deep dive into the three types of transition: medical, legal, and social. Here is an overview of some of the characteristics and elements associated with each type of transition that the chapter explored.

Medical transition is when a transgender person undergoes either surgical intervention or hormonal intervention. It is estimated that 61% of transgender individuals transition medically, with 33% undergoing surgical intervention in particular. When it comes to surgical intervention, the procedures performed are based on gender, meaning that transgender men receive different surgical interventions than transgender women. For example, transgender men might choose to undergo a hysterectomy, male chest reconstruction, phalloplasty, metoidioplasty, or vaginectomy. A transgender woman, on the other hand, might choose to undergo an orchiectomy, tracheal shave, facial feminization surgery, voice feminization surgery, vaginoplasty, and breast augmentation. Both transgender men and transgender women might choose to undergo hormone replacement therapy, although the hormones utilized will differ. They might both also choose to undergo other nonsurgical interventions such as hair removal and voice and speech therapy. Chapter 4 explores common questions about medical transition.

Legal transition is the process of changing your name and/or gender marker. Once you have done so, the next phase of legal transition is going through what can be the very time-consuming – and in some instances cost-prohibitive – process of changing all of your current and historical documentation to reflect your current name and gender marker. Chapter 5 examines important considerations regarding legal transition.

Social transition is how you show up in the world. It is how you express your gender to those around you. It is how you dress, how you groom yourself, your chosen pronouns, and your chosen name; it can also include the creation of desired body contour without medical intervention. Chapter 6 discusses significant aspects of social transition.

Chapters 7 Through 10, "Workplace Dos and Don'ts"

In my line of work I am often met with questions regarding what people should and should not do when navigating working relationships with transgender people. I appreciate the desire to get it right, and it is my hope that Chapters 7 through 10 help individuals to get it right more often than not.

In Chapter 7 we discussed the importance of taking initiative when it comes to increasing your understanding of the transgender community. Seek out information from reliable sources, and understand that the community is growing and changing and thus you will have to continue to learn. This community is dynamic as opposed to static, so it is important that you stay abreast of changes within the community. When you are seeking out information about this community, be sure not to tap your transgender friends or colleagues for information. Teaching others is emotional labor, and those who teach should only do so because they desire to and not because they feel pressured to. Instead, rely on subject matter experts, peer-reviewed articles, well-vetted resource materials, and books like this one. It is also important that you prioritize this work prior to there being an identified problem. Many organizations wait until they have an employee transitioning in the workplace to begin the process of putting policies and procedures in place. It is important to be proactive as opposed to reactive. It is also best not to wait until someone lodges a complaint or files a grievance before you put measures in place to protect this group of employees. Take initiative and create a safe and affirming space because that is the desire of your organization and not because you have been made to by way of regulation, legislation, or litigation. In addition to being intentional in the creation of a safe and affirming work environment, your organization should also be intentional in supporting local, national, and international LGBTQ+ organizations, and be certain not to support organizations that are directly or indirectly undermining LGBTQ+ progress.

In Chapter 8 we discussed the importance of honoring chosen gender pronouns and names, recognizing that few things are more personal than the self-identification of your name and pronouns. We should work diligently to honor a person's name and pronouns both in and out of their presence. We should strive to make sure that they are referred to by chosen name and pronouns in all outward- and inward-facing communications and in all work-related databases, systems, or software. We should encourage everyone to share their name and pronouns to normalize the sharing of pronouns so that transgender people are not singled out as the only people to do so. We should understand that while we seek to create space for a person to feel comfortable sharing their pronouns with us, they might be apprehensive, and we should allow space for that and be sure not to pressure people to share things that they are not yet ready to share. We also discussed the fact that even with the best intentions you may get it wrong or drop the ball sometimes, and we explored the best ways to handle it if and when you do so.

In Chapter 9 we discussed both individuality and privacy. It is important to remember that, while this book can provide you with demographic data and statistics, every person is an individual with their own thoughts, beliefs, desires, aspirations, and worldview. As we seek to learn about the transgender community as a whole, it is important to remember that the community is comprised of millions of individuals and that individuality need not be lost to exclusive reliance on generalizations. It is also important to remember that identity is not necessarily static, meaning that it can change with time. We need to allow space for that and not take changes in self-identification as evidence of dishonesty or confusion. Also, recall that your transgender coworkers may be uncomfortable sharing about their transition or other aspects of their identity. We should never pressure someone to share with us. Sharing that you are transgender can have real-world implications and we should not pressure someone to place themselves in a position that is potentially unsafe. Also, know that being a member of a historically marginalized group does not in and of itself make you immune to harboring big-oted views. It is entirely possible for a transgender person to hold views that are detrimental to the transgender community as a whole, which is part and parcel of why it is so important to seek varied and nuanced opinions and not to place all of your confidence in the beliefs of one individual.

In Chapter 10 we discussed the importance of having robust policies and procedures related to the LGBTQ+ community more broadly and the transgender community more specifically. It is important that you are responsive to any claims of bullying or harassment being experienced by transgender employees, and your organization must have a zero-tolerance policy for bullying and harassment that details persistent misgendering or deadnaming as a form of bullying or harassment. It is also very important that you afford employees an opportunity to learn about the LGBTQ+ community broadly and the transgender community specifically. Often, harmful behaviors are rooted in a lack of proper education and tools. The onus is on the organization to ensure access to the necessary education and tools to be an ally in the workplace to transgender colleagues. It is also very important that you not allow the belief that you only have a small number of LGBTQ+ employees to lessen the vigor with which you seek to create a safe space for these employees. And while I feel this should go without saying, let me say it one more time to be abundantly clear: please allow individuals to use whatever bathroom, locker room, or changing facility that they are comfortable with.

Chapter 11, "What If My Question Wasn't Answered?"

In Chapter 11 we focused on how you should go about determining whether you should ask your transgender colleague questions about their transition and lived experiences. There are many things you need to take into consideration, including the necessity of obtaining the information. Do you really need to know the answer or are you simply trying to satisfy your curiosity? Is the question work related? Is the question appropriate given the nature of the relationship? Is there a power differential that needs to be considered? Is the person a subject matter expert and, if so, do they wish to utilize their expertise to answer these types of questions in the workplace? Stated differently, you should err on the side of not asking your transgender coworker questions, as opposed to trying to satisfy your curiosity.

Putting Your Allyship into Practice

As we consider the information shared in this book, we understand that the transgender community is in need of our allyship in the workplace. It is this understanding that should inform our behavior, policy, and procedures.

Meaningful and sustained allyship does not happen accidentally. So as this book comes to a close, I want you to set your intentions and formulate your commitments. True allyship exists outside of the need for personal gain and/or attention. That said, what can you contribute to the workplace that will positively impact the work experience of your transgender colleagues? How can you help to foster a safe and affirming work environment? Reading this book was a great first step. Now, on to step two: putting this information into practice.

10 Things I've Learned During My Personal Journey of Transition

If you've made it this far, you are the real MVP. I know that was a lot of information for you to process in all of the chapters. When writing this book, some things were important to me. I wanted to share glimpses of my story but did not want it to read as a memoir. I wanted to make sure that the book was full of helpful information you could apply that was supported by data instead of just sharing personal anecdotes. I stayed true to that vision in writing this book, but I found that when I was finished, some things had been left unsaid.

This appendix is meant to bridge the gap between my desire to ensure this is a practical resource and my desire to allow you to take a more personal look at my feelings on this subject. To this end, I have written this appendix. That is not to say that this information cannot also be used to inform your behavior, but it is meant to convey that this section will read a little more like a sharing of my thoughts and feelings than the book's main content. I hope you find this to be just as valuable.

1. Sexual Orientation and Gender Identity Can Be Fluid

It became apparent to me with time that who I know myself to be today and who I will know myself to be tomorrow might not be the same person. There are many reasons this might be the case for someone. For some, they don't have the language to describe themselves accurately, so they refer to themselves using their limited vocabulary, and once exposed to additional terminology, the way that they refer to themselves changes. That was definitely the case for me.

When I was very young, I viewed myself as straight, not knowing that there was any other option. My attractions were not consistent with that, but I didn't have the language to describe myself otherwise. Eventually, I learned that individuals could be gay, and that was the title that seemed to better fit me. I realized, though, that my attraction was not necessarily just to women exclusively; I didn't have the language to say that either. It wasn't until I was introduced to the term "bisexual" that I referred to myself as such. But that wasn't the ending; with time I came to realize that bisexual didn't quite tell the whole story and that while I do have the capacity to be attracted to both men and women, I also possess the capacity to be attracted to individuals who do not identify exclusively as men or women. Once I came to that realization, I began to refer to myself as pansexual. But that, too, was temporary because I've come to realize that while I do have the capacity to be attracted to individuals of any gender identity, I would not go as far as to say that gender does not matter to me and has no bearing on my level of attraction. Armed with that information and additional terminology, I now consider myself omnisexual. Will I identify as omnisexual for the rest of my life? Maybe. But I might also find that something else more accurately describes my experience, and if that is the case, I will adjust my language. In this example my experience of attraction did not change, but my ability to characterize that experience changed with time.

There are also situations in which a person's actual experience of attraction changes with time. You may be attracted to one gender at one juncture in your life and another gender at another. You may find that you have the ability to be attracted to individuals of any gender identity at one juncture in your life and that you no longer have that capacity at another. That is OK. Sexual orientation is static for many people and does not change, but that is not the case for everyone, and the fact that it is not the experience for everyone does not lessen the veracity of the experience.

Similarly, my gender identity has changed with time. When I was younger, I identified as a girl. I didn't have knowledge of or the language to describe feeling different from other little girls I knew. So based on my limited access to language, I referred to myself as a tomboy. As I got older and I began to explore my attraction to women, I made the common mistake of conflating sexual orientation and gender identity and I thought that my gender identity was an artifact of the fact that I was a lesbian. During this period, I referred to myself as a stud. It wasn't until much later that I realized that my experience of gender was

191

Appendix

different from other lesbians. One thing I had in common with lesbians was that I was female-bodied and attracted to women, but that seemed to be the extent of it because where they still felt very much like women, that was not my experience. I did not feel like I was a woman despite being in a female body.

I was not only an adult but well into adulthood before I began to use the word "transgender" to describe myself. It took me a long time to embrace that language, and I struggled with feeling as though I needed to make the realization that I was transgender more palatable, not just for others but for myself. So I tried really hard to normalize my experience. I wanted people to understand that I was just like them, that my life was just like theirs, that my family was just like theirs, that I was not an anomaly but that I was normal. I realize now that I was struggling with my own internalized transphobia. I did not feel fully "normal," so I tried desperately to convince others and myself that I was normal.

What I really want you to understand from sharing this is that at no point in time was I trying to be dishonest or disingenuous. At no point in time was I trying to pull the wool over someone's eyes or lead someone astray. Quite the contrary, actually – in that all the while, what I was trying to do was to really figure out how best to describe and explain my lived experience. But it may have been a little confusing for someone who was watching from the sideline. My understanding of myself has evolved over the years. Based on everything that I know about myself at this time, I would describe myself as a transgender man

Appendix

who is omnisexual. There may come a time when something else more accurately describes my experience, and should that be the case, I will change the way that I refer to myself. If that happens, please know that I meant every word of this paragraph as I wrote it. But I reserve the right to change my mind or to become more deeply aware of my truth, and if that happens, I will work to embrace myself as I know myself to be.

2. Sensitivity to Misgendering and Deadnaming Can Change with Time

I was in my 20s when I realized that I was transgender. Looking back, I recognize that I have always been different, but I didn't know what that meant. Once I understood that I was transgender, I was terrified of the possible ramifications. How would I be perceived? Would I lose the love and support of those closest to me? And we won't even begin to discuss the fears that I had that were rooted in my religious upbringing. I was afraid, but not only was I afraid, I was confused because my experience at the time seemed unique to me.

Even though I identified as transgender, I did not experience the gender dysphoria many other transgender people experienced. I felt I was in the wrong body, but I did not experience distress associated with that realization. And because of that, it didn't bother me if someone utilized my given name or the pronouns that were consistent with the sex that I was assigned at birth. I remember in many presentations explaining to participants that they could refer to me as she or he, and either was fine, I did not become offended, and I didn't experience dysphoria associated with using either of those pronouns.

Over time though, I began to notice a shift in that every time someone referred to me utilizing he/him pronouns, I experienced a small twinge of joy. I didn't really know what that meant, and to be honest, I didn't give it very much thought. I just kind of smiled and moved on. However, as time progressed, something began to shift even more. Not only was it a positive experience when someone referred to me utilizing masculine pronouns, but it began to be an uncomfortable experience when someone referred to me utilizing feminine pronouns. And with time, that experience progressed such that when someone referred to me as she or her, I began to experience discomfort, and over time, that discomfort grew to be the experience of dysphoria, which was new to me because that had not been my experience prior. More and more, it felt as though referring to me as she and her was actually harmful. It went from being something that I rarely noticed to being something that impacted me deeply.

Now, this didn't happen to me overnight. This progression slowly took place over the course of 10 years or so until I eventually reached a place where I experienced significant dysphoria every time someone referred to me as she or her. It was jarringly painful. It was as if the wind was being knocked out of me. It was as if I was being attacked and was totally defenseless. I want to make sure you understand that If you met me 10 years ago, I likely would have introduced myself to you using my dead name (because it wasn't my dead name yet), and I would have told you that you could utilize whatever pronouns you liked because it really made no difference to me. But now, nothing could be further from the truth. Being misgendered is painful for me, and being referred to using my dead name or really having to interface with my dead name at all for any reason is particularly distressing for me. Was I being dishonest during all of those presentations many years ago? No. But if an audience member asked me the same questions today, they would get an entirely different set of answers.

3. Your Experience of Dysphoria Can Change with Time

I touched on this a bit in the previous section, but I just want to make sure that I'm really clearly explaining that the experience of dysphoria can be different for different people at different times in their journey. There were things that did not cause me dysphoria in the past that absolutely cause me dysphoria now. There are situations that were particularly impactful for me a year or two ago that are less impactful for me now, and it's probably not the case that my current experience will be my forever experience. For example, I have experienced various types and levels of dysphoria as it relates to my body over the years. There were times that I have desperately wanted top surgery, and there have been times when it has been the furthest thing from my mind. Interestingly enough, if I were to have top surgery at this juncture, it would likely be to pull myself into greater alignment instead of attempting to escape significant dysphoria.

4. Systemic Slights Can Be Just as Painful as Individualized or Personal Ones

When a person gets it wrong, they are uniquely positioned to apologize, make the correction, and behave differently in the future. For this reason, in some ways, I find it easier to handle when an individual gets it wrong than when a system gets it wrong. When a system gets it wrong, it's often the case that you cannot find a quick and painless solution. For example, you might work for an organization where your dead name is populated in automated reports. Often, it takes time, resources, and a desire on the part of the organization for there to actually be a change on a systemic level, and not all organizations have an appetite for that type of change or see the benefit.

Systems matter. We cannot direct all of our effort toward training people and not place comparable effort into improving systems. We need both. We need to educate people, and we must review and continuously upgrade and improve our systems, our software, our databases, our policies and procedures. We must address the systemic as well as the individual if we want people to truly feel safe and affirmed in the workplace.

5. Safety Is a Legitimate Concern for Our Community

Sadly, there are people with very strong negative emotions concerning the very existence of transgender individuals. The frequency with which I hear and see negative commentary about the transgender community has increased significantly in the past several years. We have become the focus of legislation that villainizes us and portrays us as predators and people who seek to do harm. With this increase in transphobic rhetoric, there has also been an increase in open disdain for our community.

It is, unfortunately, the case that there are individuals who seek to do us harm. It's important to understand that outing a transgender person can literally place them in harm's way. It is important that you be sensitive to the fact that a person may be open about their transgender identity in certain aspects of their life but not in others. They may be open about their transgender identity in certain circumstances but not in others. And it is important to honor their choosing because it is very possibly the case that they have made this decision in an attempt to keep themselves safe.

One way to honor the transgender people in your life is to take time to learn their goals as it relates to community acceptance. Do they desire people to know that they are transgender? Is being transgender an important part of their identity? Would they prefer that their being transgender be hidden? How would they like you to refer to them? Is this desire consistent across environments? For example, do they want you to use their chosen name at all times, or might there be instances in which they would prefer you use their deadname (i.e., around family, at church, when enjoying a night on the town, or around strangers)? If they are misgendered in your presence, do they want you to correct the person, pretend you didn't hear it, or do something entirely different? If someone expresses a romantic interest in them, do they want you to mention that they are transgender, or would they prefer to get to know that person and share this information with them at a later time? If you are in a public space and they need to use the restroom, do they want you to accompany them so that there is a buddy system? If someone asks them directly if they are transgender, do they want you to intervene? If someone asks you if they are transgender, do they want you to answer the question, ignore the question, deflect the question, or send the person to them directly? These are just a small number of circumstances that could escalate quickly and become potentially dangerous for a transgender person. It is imperative that you have a sense of how you can best support them should a situation become hostile.

6. Privilege Is Still a Thing

Privilege is an uncomfortable topic for many people. Something about the word "privilege" elicits a visceral response for some. Despite this, we must discuss it, and I think it is important to address it head-on. First, we must be willing to acknowledge that privilege exists. Privilege is associated with proximity to the majority, and proximity to power. If you are cisgender, you experience privilege that a transgender person is not able to easily access. If you are a heterosexual, you experience privilege that a gay person is not able to easily access.

Is privilege a bad thing? No. It is what you do with your privilege that matters. Do you help others? Do you stand up for what is right? Do you do everything in your power to create opportunities for individuals who are members of historically marginalized groups? You have privilege. What are you doing with it?

Now, to be clear, I recognize that I, too, have privilege. I know it may seem a bit odd for a Black, transgender person to say they have privilege, but hear me out. I have a PhD, and the fact that I have attained that level of education allows me access to spaces that others are unable to access. Not only that, but my thoughts, opinions, and feedback are given a certain level of credence as an artifact of that credentialing. Does this mean that life is easy for me? No. But understanding my own privilege means that I both recognize and acknowledge that it could be harder.

To be honest, I sometimes feel that people who are members of historically marginalized groups lose sight of the privilege they do, in fact, possess, and when we do that, we lose the ability to share that privilege with others. I encourage you to take time to reflect on what privilege you hold and how you can share it with others.

7. Being a Member of This Community Doesn't Mean You Don't Make Mistakes

I often meet people who allow their fear of messing up to get in the way of their allyship. Sometimes people are so afraid of doing it wrong that they choose to do nothing at all. This fear is an artifact of an unrealistic expectation of perfection, the belief that it is possible to get it right 100% of the time. Is there someone out there who never messes up? Maybe. Have I met that person? No. Am I that person? Certainly not. I'm a transgender man, and even I mess up.

So let's normalize the fact that you're going to get it wrong sometimes, and that is OK. What's not OK is not trying at all because you're afraid that you might mess up. Do not fall into that trap. I can only speak for myself, but I prefer that you try and get it wrong from time to time than that you stand by idly and not put forth an honest effort. I personally find it relatively easy to extend grace to someone whom I know is truly trying.

As we discussed before, if you get it wrong, self-correct, apologize, and move on to try again. As with any other behavior, practice makes progress, and the more practice you have doing it right, the less often you will make mistakes, and the more often you will experience the positive reinforcement of having a member of a historically marginalized community feel affirmed. We are all still learning; no matter if you are a novice or a subject matter expert, none of us know it all. So let's aspire to get it right and apologize and correct if we get it wrong.

8. A Transgender Person May Never Be Able to "Pass," and Passing Should Not Be the Meter Stick

I'll use myself as an example for this one. I am a transgender man, but at this juncture in my journey of transition, I am not able to pass as a cisgender man. I am currently on hormone therapy, but I've not been taking testosterone long enough or consistently enough to have begun to grow much in the way of facial hair. My voice has dropped a little, but it's still not particularly deep. And as of the time of this writing, I have yet to have top surgery. Add to that the fact that I have long hair and relatively feminine facial features, and you have the perfect recipe for a transgender man who is unable to pass as a cisgender man. Does that make me any less transgender? No. My experience is just as valid. My voice is just as important. My lens and perspective are just as needed as someone who is completely able to pass.

Additionally, this might be difficult for some people to understand, but believe it or not, being able to pass isn't always the actual end goal for a transgender person. Some individuals don't feel the need to be able to pass as cisgender and might not even try to pass. A transgender person's relationship with the entire concept of passing is just as varied and individualized as every other aspect of our lives. There are some who want nothing more than to be able to pass as cisgender. There are some who really couldn't care less about being able to pass as cisgender. There are some who find it to be important to varying degrees at different times in their life. There are some who find it to be particularly important in certain situations, environments, or circumstances.

9. It's Hard to Hate Up Close

I have met many people over the years who have held negative beliefs about the transgender community but found it difficult to continue to espouse those beliefs after entering into a relationship with me. I'm not referencing romantic relationships but instead I'm talking about becoming acquaintances, friends, or colleagues.

I personally believe that part of the reason this is the case is because it's really easy to hate a people group when you don't actually have a personal connection to that people group. When there is distance between you and another person, it's easy to view them as a monster or a villain, but when you actually interact with them one-on-one and see that, just like you, they have hopes and dreams and aspirations and families and friends and loved ones, it becomes difficult to maintain a view of them as inferior or dangerous.

Don't get me wrong. I'm not suggesting that members of historically marginalized communities go out and befriend people who are blatantly transphobic or homophobic or racist or sexist or ageist, but what I am saying is that what I have found is that it's really difficult to maintain an inequitable value set when faced with real-life engagement with people who are different from you. So am I saying that transgender people need to go be friends with cisgender people, especially those who are transphobic? That is absolutely not what I'm saying.

What I'm actually saying is if you are cisgender and you don't know any transgender people, I hope you would consider getting to know a member of this beautiful community. You might find that your perspective changes.

10. I Don't Have to Understand You to Treat You with Dignity and Respect

Let's face it. There are times when, no matter how hard you try, you just can't quite understand another person's experience. For example, no matter how many thought experiments I might engage in, I will never truly understand what it is like to be a White heterosexual cisgender man. I can meditate on it. I can speak to as many White heterosexual cisgender men as I can find. I can read about the experience, but at the end of the day, I will never fully be able to understand. And that is OK.

We must not make understanding a prerequisite for treating one another with dignity and respect. If I were to be completely honest with you, there are many people I do not understand. I do not understand why they vote the way that they vote, why they believe the things they believe, why they espouse the things they espouse, but none of that is an excuse for maltreatment.

There are some who believe that respect is earned. I disagree wholeheartedly. I personally believe that respect is the minimum. It is to be given freely, and if we treat one another with respect, we might find that there are things we can align on after all, even if that thing is simply the belief that everyone should be treated with dignity and respect.

So if you have read this book and there are still some things that you don't quite understand, that is OK. You might never reach a place where it all makes complete sense to you, and it's best to reconcile yourself with that because unrealistic expectations are harmful to all of us.

Acknowledgments

I want to thank my son, Kevin; without him, I would never have strived so hard. May your generation right the wrongs of my generation. To my parents, who, despite societal and religious pressure to the contrary, found it in their hearts to love and accept me. To my wife, who is my biggest cheerleader and gives me a pep talk whenever I feel less than enough. To my bonus kids, thank you for letting me love your mother. I want to give a big thank you to Wiley for being at the forefront of such an important discussion. I want to thank Victoria Savanh for finding me and asking me to write a book. Who knew it would be this magical?! To Kelly Talbot, we did it! You are the best editor on either side of the Mississippi. To everyone who supports my work, thank you.

Thank you to all the companies out there that bring me in to train your employees. To every organization that has brought me in to keynote, thank you. Thank you to everyone who follows me on social media and has been rooting me on. To everyone I have ever worked with who has embraced me in the fullness of who I am, thank you. To everyone who has gotten it right and even to a couple of people who have gotten it wrong, thank you for helping to shape my character and solidify my trajectory. To every member of the absolutely beautiful transgender community, I see you, and I affirm you. May you find peace, purpose, and restoration in every aspect of your life, including the workplace.

About the Author

Dr. A.C. Fowlkes is the Chief Executive Officer of Fowlkes Consulting, an LGBTQ+ sensitivity and transgender inclusion consulting firm. He is a clinical psychologist and has worked in diversity and inclusion for over 15 years. He is an LGBTQ+ Subject Matter Expert and Thought Leader. His passion for LGBTQ+ sensitivity and inclusion is palpable and has resulted in him becoming a highly sought-after speaker and consultant. He has provided training and consultation in multiple settings, including the financial sector, the aerospace sector, the prison system, institutions of higher education, hospital systems, and luxury retail. As a transgender man himself, Dr. Fowlkes has a profound appreciation for the impact (both blatant and subtle) of diversity, equity, and inclusion in the workplace. Dr. Fowlkes is a *Forbes* contributor, where he writes about LGBTQ+ sensitivity, transgender inclusion, and allyship. He served as the inaugural Director of Diversity, Inclusion, and Belonging at his alma mater, Virginia State University. He is noted as the first out Black transgender man to be in the role of psychiatric hospital leader in the United States. He is a proud member of the board of directors for the Trevor Project. And he was recently named a Top Voice by LinkedIn and selected as one of the Top 10 Voices to follow in LGBTQIA+ in the United States and Canada.

Index